11+ VERBAL REASONING TESTS

for GL Assessment

Practice Papers

with Detailed Answers & Challenging Words List

VOLUME II

Ages 10-11

ABOUT THIS BOOK

This book contains **3 full 11+ Verbal Reasoning Practice Test Papers** aimed at students aged 10-11 preparing for the **11 Plus and other secondary school entrance exams** containing the verbal reasoning element.

Each Practice Test Paper consists of **80 unrepeated questions** that are representative of the types of questions used in **actual exams set by the GL board**.

Students can fill their standard answers in by hand in this book in the spaces provided **OR** they can use our **free, infinite-use <u>SELF-MARKING</u> Multiple-Choice Online Answer Pages** on our website.

At the end of the book, students, parents, and teachers will find
◊   Complete **Answers** for all the questions
◊   Complete **Detailed Explanations** showing why the correct solutions are the correct solutions
◊   A **List** of particularly **challenging words** used in the tests

HOW TO USE THIS BOOK

We recommend that
◊   Students attempt these tests in a **quiet environment**
◊   Students work through these tests **in order** (as their **difficulty level increases** each time)
◊   These tests are used to **identify the areas** where students excel and those which they might find challenging
◊   The marks obtained by students in these tests are used as an **indication** of their progress

<u>PLEASE NOTE</u> that all the questions in these Tests have only **one correct answer**. However, with certain question types, **it is possible for students to arrive at the correct answer via routes of reasoning** *other* than those set out in the explanations.

GOOD LUCK!

Access your FREE
SELF-MARKING
ANSWER PAGES HERE! https://bit.ly/2SNEHnv

Find more FREE
EDUCATIONAL &
EDUTAINMENT
Resources HERE! https://bit.ly/2yusdKP

Published by STP Books
An imprint of Swot Tots Publishing Ltd
Kemp House
152-160 City Road
London EC1V 2NX

www.swottotspublishing.com

Typeset, cover design, and inside concept design by Swot Tots Publishing Ltd.

British Library Cataloguing-in-Publication Data. A catalogue record for this book is available from the British Library.

ISBN 978-1-912956-14-2

CONTENTS

NOTES FOR CANDIDATES

WHAT TO DO BEFORE, WHILE & AFTER
COMPLETING YOUR VERBAL REASONING PRACTICE TEST PAPERS

BEFORE you attempt a Practice Test Paper

- Decide which answer format you want to use.
- **DO NOT** look at either the questions or the multiple-choice online answer pages (if you are using them) **before** you start doing the Practice Test Paper.

WHILE you do a Practice Test Paper

- Work as quickly and as carefully as you can to finish all 80 questions in 50 minutes.
- If you come across a question that you cannot answer quickly, leave it and go back to it at the end if you have time.
- Remember that it **sometimes helps to work things out in writing in rough**, rather than trying to do it all in your head.
- Make sure you provide an answer for **ALL** the questions, even if you are unsure or are simply making an educated guess!

AFTER you finish a Practice Test Paper

- Using the **Answers** section of this book, mark your answers with your parent.
- You can also mark them on your own – just make sure you're being honest with yourself.
- Have another go at the questions you have got wrong, or couldn't do.
- Go through the relevant sections of the **Explanations** that are in this book. You can do this with your parent, or on your own if you wish.

& FINALLY...

Don't be discouraged if you make mistakes.
Remember: it is by making mistakes that we learn.
Also, once you have mastered how to answer the different types of verbal reasoning questions, the best thing you can do to prepare for your exams is to practise, practise, practise – and then practise some more.
The more practice you have, the faster and more accurate you will become.

Last, but not least...

Good luck!

PRACTICE TEST PAPER 4

This is a **50 minute test**. Work as quickly, but as accurately, as you can.

Remember: you can also use our **_free self-marking online multiple-choice answer pages_** that you can use over and over again, plus you'll get an instant test report when you have finished that provides your overall score out of 80.

Simply visit our website here: **https://bit.ly/2SNEHnv** and click on the appropriate button.

The number codes for three of the four following words are listed randomly below. Work out the **code** to answer the questions.

> **DART   DARE   FAIR   FEAR**
> **6523   1234   6273**

1.   Find the code for **FAIR**.   _____

2.   What does the code **4735** stand for?   _____

3.   What does the code **2623** stand for?   _____

The number codes for three of the four following words are listed randomly below. Work out the **code** to answer the questions.

> **CRAW   ACHE   CROW   ACRE**
> **4279   4289   8456**

4.   Find the code for **ACRE**.   _____

5.   Find the code for **HARE**.   _____

6.   What does the code **9726** stand for?   _____

In the following, find the **two words** – one from each set – which are the closest in meaning.

Example: *(**sound** healthy ill)*   *(**noise** quiet whisper)*

7.   (thin   squeeze   fit)   (jog   exercise   healthy)

8.   (near   far   beside)   (approach   distance   range)

9.   (kind   type   species)   (mean   unkind   nice)

10. (itch   scratch   nervous)   (calm   placid   twitchy)

11. (king   queen   earl)   (countess   emperor   prince)

For the questions below, find the **two words** – one from each set – which are the most opposite in meaning.

Example: *(funny **happy** sad)*   *(sunken **depressed** bent)*

12. (there   real   hard)   (mind   creative   imaginary)

13. (ancient   myth   treasure)   (relic   youthful   aged)

14. (eat   breakfast   brown)   (supper   orange   toast)

15. (spice   food   eat)   (fork   fast   quick)

16. (east   sun   rise)   (dawn   elevate   descend)

In the questions below, each letter stands for a number. Work out the **letter solution** to each sum.

Example: *A = 5, B = 3, C = 2, D = 6, E = 11*   *A x B – C² x C ÷ E =*   __*C*__

17. A = 4, B = 24, C = 6, D = 2, E = 3   B x E ÷ C x D = _____

18. A = 3, B = 4, C = 18, D = 6, E = 12   E ÷ D x C ÷ A = _____

19. A = 3, B = 4, C = 6, D = 12   2C ÷ (D ÷ B) = _____

20. A = 1, B = 3, C = 5, D = 7   (4C + A) ÷ D = _____

21. A = 1, B = 4, C = 6, D = 7, E = 8   5D ÷ (A + B) = _____

In each sentence below, a **four-letter word** is hidden at the end of one word and the start of the next. Find the hidden word.

Example: *"I always <u>wan</u>ted to be a doctor," Sita said.*   __*swan*__

22. The only person who managed to solve the problem was Julia.   _____

23. "Your glasses are in their case," Khaled said to his wife.   _____

24. Toby couldn't recall his last argument.   _____

25. "Have you seen Papa in his new jacket?" said Mabel.   _____

26. We haven't been to the cinema for ages.   _____

For each of the questions below, find a **word** that completes the third pair of words so that it follows the same pattern as the first two pairs.

Example: site   sit   cute   cut   pipe   ?   __*pip*__

27. star   rats   warts   straw   bard   ?   _____

28. indigo   din   endanger   den   entrance   ?   _____

29. bubble   blue   fumble   flue   cuddle   ?   _____

30. bale   able   care   acre   gore   ?   _____

31. cheating   chant   freaking   frank   creaking   ?   _____

In the next questions, choose **two words**, one from each set of brackets, which complete the sentence in the most sensible way.

Example: **Meat** is to (**_food_** animal pet) as **juice** is to (orange **_drink_** sugary).

32. **Heat** is to (hot hate sun) as **meat** is to (food vegetables mate).

33. **Cavalry** is to (horsemen troop ride) as **infantry** is to (banners march artillery).

34. **News** is to (paper magazine report) as **note** is to (letter jot book).

35. **Prize** is to (win trophy cup) as **gift** is to (absent receive ribbon).

36. **Stride** is to (long giant leagues) as **crawl** is to (swim totter baby).

37. $12 \times 4 - 3 \div 9 = 14 \div 2 + 3 - (\,?\,)$ _____

38. $6 + 5 - 3 \times 4 = 11 \times 2 + 9 + (\,?\,)$ _____

39. $16 - 5 \times 4 = 17 \times 3 - 10 + (\,?\,)$ _____

40. $64 \div 8 + 5 = 3 \times 15 \div 5 + (\,?\,)$ _____

41. $39 - 6 \div 11 = 26 - 5 \div (\,?\,)$ _____

A B C D E F G H I J K L M N O P Q R S T U V W X Y Z

42.   If the code for **FORD** is **ULIW**, what does **XLIV** stand for?   _____

43.   If the code for **CHILD** is **ALGPB**, what does **MVBIP** stand for?   _____

44.   If the code for **TABLE** is **YDJRV**, what does **JDRRVY** stand for?   _____

45.   If the code for **SANDY** is **OXLCY**, what is the code for **EARTH**?   _____

46.   If the code for **PASTE** is **UEVVF**, what is the code for **ROARS**?   _____

47.   54,   52,   49,   45,   _____

48.   3,   4,   7,   11,   18,   _____

49.   144,   120,   96,   72,   _____

50.   3,   6,   7,   5,   11,   4,   _____

51.   1,   4,   9,   16,   _____

In the next questions, the words in the second set follow the same pattern as the words in the first set. Work out the rule to find the **missing word** to complete the second set.

Example: pour (pod) bud   leaf (?) sit   **let**

52. happy (part) sort   ports (?) barn   torn

53. item (mile) left   leap (?) odes   plod

54. mall (tell) rate   beat (?) much   chat

55. earl (loft) foot   open (?) sore   nose

56. slim (low) wood   step (?) poll   top

57. pass (last) tool   with (?) soup   pits

58. score (coal) all   sport (?) urn   pour

In each of the following, find the **two words** – one from the first group and one from the second group – which make a proper new word when combined.

Example: (**bit** part bite)   (ton **ten** tan)

59. (fat big thin)   (him her us)

60. (crumb drop bit)   (head lead led)

61. (gum fang tooth)   (glue paste stick)

62. (a as so)   (line tack side)

63. (ma pa gran)   (par per for)

Carefully read the following information, then **answer the questions** below.

64. John, Harry, Alan, Mark, and Stephen were all given presents for their birthdays by their friends. John and Mark both received a football, and Harry, Mark, and Stephen had a DVD. All of them except Mark got a video game. Stephen and Alan were each given a book.

Who received the **most** presents?   _____

65. Charlie wants to invite a few of his friends to his birthday party. As none of them are free at the weekends, Charlie has to have his party on a weekday. However, they all have various activities on different evenings of the week. Greg can only manage Monday and Thursday because of football training. Both Simon and Harry are free every evening except Monday. David says he prefers Friday, but is free on Monday and Tuesday as well. Boris can only attend on Wednesday or Friday evening.

On **which day** can the **largest** number of Charlie's friends attend his party?

_____

In the following questions, the numbers in each group are related in the same way. Find the **missing number** in the third group.

Example: 9 (10) 1   4 (7) 3   8 (?) 8   __16__

---

66.   11 (66) 3   12 (96) 4   9 (?) 4   _____

67.   11 (64) 3   7 (4) 5   9 (?) 2   _____

68.   26 (15) 15   42 (34) 12   20 (?) 11   _____

69.   3 (13) 2   5 (34) 3   4 (?) 3   _____

70.   7 (4) 49   3 (11) 42   6 (?) 54   _____

In each of the following, find **one letter** which can be removed from the first word and added to the second word to make two new proper words.

Example: SCALE   ALL   __C__

---

71.   BOMB   RAP   _____

72.   OWN   SADDLE   _____

73.   CULT   BET   _____

74.   GRID   REIN   _____

75.   LEAST   HOP   _____

In the questions below, find the **pair of letters** that most sensibly completes the analogy. Use the alphabet to help you.

Example: **AB** is to **FG** as **QR** is to (UV **VW** WX VU UX).

A B C D E F G H I J K L M N O P Q R S T U V W X Y Z

76.   **FD** is to **JX** as **MX** is to (QS SQ RQ RS QR).

77.   **AB** is to **ZY** as **LM** is to (MN ON NO MO OM).

78.   **DV** is to **DW** as **TU** is to (UV TW VT TV VU).

79.   **AZ** is to **EV** as **EV** is to (FI FR IR IE VE).

80.   **FP** is to **MK** as **VC** is to (DX CX BX CY CZ).

TOTAL SCORE: / 80

END OF PRACTICE TEST PAPER 4

PRACTICE TEST PAPER 5

This is a **50 minute test**. Work as quickly, but as accurately, as you can.

Remember: you can also use our *__free self-marking online multiple-choice answer pages__* that you can use over and over again, plus you'll get an instant test report when you have finished that provides your overall score out of 80.

Simply visit our website here: **https://bit.ly/2SNEHnv** and click on the appropriate button.

For the following, find the **number** that continues each sequence in the best way.

Example: 2,   4,   6,   8,   10,   12

1.   3, 8, 6, 11, 9, _____

2.   39, 41, 38, 43, 37, _____

3.   2, 1, 3, 3, 4, 5, _____

4.   49, 37, 47, 39, 45, 41, _____

5.   5, 6, 11, 17, 28, _____

6.   5, 1, 10, 6, 15, _____

For each of the following, find the **letter** that completes both sets of letter clusters to make two proper words.

Example: jo ( ) ag   crum ( ) low   b

7.   her ( ) men   hell ( ) ats   _____

8.   whiz ( ) one   buz ( ) any   _____

9.   den ( ) end   ten ( ) ask   _____

10.   dra ( ) here   cla ( ) ill   _____

11.   you ( ) ice   pipe ( ) ink   _____

In the next questions, choose **two words**, one from each set of brackets, which complete the sentence in the most sensible way.

Example: **Meat** *is to (**food** animal pet) as **juice** is to (orange **drink** sugary).*

12.   **Lead** is to (follow metal pipe) as **order** is to (obey rank arrange).

13.   **Whale** is to (ocean mammal school) as **snake** is to (egg slither reptile).

14.   **Coward** is to (timid villain scoundrel) as **hero** is to (soldier brave courage).

15.   **Edit** is to (tide diet correct) as **time** is to (emit clock tell).

16.   **Sole** is to (shoe fish soul) as **sale** is to (auction sail bargain).

In the next questions, find the **missing number** which completes the sum correctly.

Example: $17 - 3 \div 2 = 6 \times 6 - 8 \div (\,?\,)$ __4__

17. $41 \times 2 - 1 \div 9 = 7 \times 6 + 12 \div (\,?\,)$ _____

18. $23 - 7 \times 2 \div 4 = 15 \div 5 + 11 - (\,?\,)$ _____

19. $28 + 8 \div 12 = 63 \div 3 \div (\,?\,)$ _____

20. $64 \div 8 \times 3 - 1 = 9 \div 3 \times 2 + (\,?\,)$ _____

21. $34 - 4 \div 6 = 75 \div 3 - 15 - (\,?\,)$ _____

22. $72 \div 9 \times 2 - 1 = 25 + 8 \div 3 + (\,?\,)$ _____

In the following, find the **two words** – one from each set – which are the closest in meaning.

Example: *(**sound** healthy ill)   (**noise** quiet whisper)*

23.   (waft aroma drift)   (putrid rank odour)

24.   (boat pier dock)   (wood cut mast)

25.   (volume knob part)   (loud quiet tome)

26.   (kind helpful grateful)   (please gently thankful)

27.   (labels organised bookmark)   (chaotic messy orderly)

28.   (bother bug nag)   (mare donkey foal)

29.   Five friends enjoy eating fish. Sally's favourite is plaice, but she also likes halibut, cod, and salmon. Maurice never eats salmon, and only likes plaice and halibut. Only John, Mary, and Michael enjoy tuna. Mary and John never eat cod or salmon.

If all these statements are true, only one of the sentences below **cannot be true**. Which one?

A.   Three of them never eat salmon.   ☐

B.   Cod is the least popular.   ☐

C.   Mary eats halibut.   ☐

D.   Maurice and John both like tuna.   ☐

E.   Sally likes at least three kinds of fish.   ☐

30.   Five students were short-listed for form captain. In the final vote Molly received five more votes than Andy. Lindsay got four fewer votes than Molly. David and Petra won the same number of votes. Andy and David were each chosen by five of their classmates.

If all these statements are true, only one of the sentences below **must be true**. Which one?

A.   Molly received eleven votes.   ☐

B.   David got six fewer votes than Molly.   ☐

C.   There were thirty-four children in the class.   ☐

D.   David and Andy were friends.   ☐

E.   Lindsay received six votes.   ☐

For each of the questions below, find a **word** that completes the third pair of words so that it follows the same pattern as the first two pairs.

Example: site   sit   cute   cut   pipe   ?   **pip**

31.   absorbed   bed   offered   fed   aligned   ?   _____

32.   derived   drive   coursed   curse   lounged   ?   _____

33.   tramp   part   ported   drop   married   ?   _____

34.   breaded   bad   speared   sad   treated   ?   _____

35.   courted   curt   founded   fund   jousted   ?   _____

In the questions below, each letter stands for a number. Work out the **letter solution** to each sum.

Example: A = 5, B = 3, C = 2, D = 6, E = 11   A x B − C² x C ÷ E =   **C**

36.   A = 7, B = 5, C = 13, D = 25, E = 10   D + B − C − A =   _____

37.   A = 2, B = 4, C = 5, D = 6, E = 9   (ED − B) ÷ AC =   _____

38.   A = 8, B = 2, C = 13, D = 6, E = 15   A ÷ B + E − D =   _____

39.   A = 3, B = 4, C = 6, D = 8   (AB + AD) ÷ C =   _____

40.   A = 25, B = 30, C = 2, D = 12, E = 20   A − E x D − B =   _____

41.   A = 3, B = 4, C = 6, D = 7   (C² + B) ÷ (A + D) =   _____

Three of the words in each of the following lists are related in some way. For each question, find the **two words** which do not belong.

*Example: leg   arm   **heart**   hand   **lungs**__*

42.   study   show   examine   display   inspect

43.   snakes and ladders   chess   Scrabble   draughts   backgammon

44.   a   me   the   an   she

45.   quickly   slowly   sped   hastily   rate

46.   graceful   elegance   grace   refinement   polished

For the following, find the **word** from the list of words given that has a similar meaning to the words in both pairs of brackets.

*Example: (shop market) (save reserve)   buy keep **store** gather collect*

47.   (run trot) (nudge prod)   canter remind prompt jog gallop

48.   (grill brown) (honour salute)   pledge toast barbecue bake drink

49.   (line tier) (quarrel argument)   row queue series dispute tiff

50.   (actors company) (throw hurl)   troupe players cast fling pitch

51.   (fashion vogue) (method way)   trend craze mode fad means

52.   (pie pastry) (sour bitter)   sharp flan acid sarcastic tart

For each of the following questions, find the **term** that continues the sequence in the most logical way. Use the alphabet to help you.

*Example: 2K,   3M,   4O,   5Q,   **6S***

A B C D E F G H I J K L M N O P Q R S T U V W X Y Z

53.   TA, QD, NG, KJ, HM, _____

54.   BDF, CBG, DZH, EXI, _____

55.   W, V, T, Q, M, _____

56.   9B, 7Y, 5V, 3S, _____

57.   Ab2, Cc4, Ed6, Ge8, _____

58.   ZH, WL, TP, QT, NX, _____

59.   A, G, F, D, K, A, P, _____

In each sentence below, a **four-letter word** is hidden at the end of one word and the start of the next. Find the hidden word.

Example: "I always <u>wanted to</u> be a doctor," Sita said.   <u>swan</u>

60.   A big lumbering giant came into view.   _____

61.   I followed the man until he disappeared.   _____

62. These enigmatic markings are extremely old. _____

63. Ahmed is always careful when using knives. _____

64. The kitten tried to catch the butterfly. _____

> For the questions below, find the **two words** – one from each set – which are the most opposite in meaning.
>
> *Example:* (funny **happy** sad)   (sunken **depressed** bent)

65. (long brief case)   (leather cover lengthy)

66. (separate component bit)   (part divide mix)

67. (entering exiting apathy)   (boardroom boredom excitement)

68. (inert insolent impotent)   (impertinent polite rude)

69. (greedy fat pig)   (gobble miserly generous)

70. (sum all complete)   (star start whole)

> Carefully read the following information, then **answer the questions** below.

71. Five children were asked which after-school activities they liked. Susan said that she enjoyed football the most, but also liked cookery, swimming, and hockey. Tarek also preferred football, but thought that swimming was great fun, too. Philip, Tom, and Julian all said that rugby and cookery were their favourites. Philip added that he liked swimming as well.

    Which activity was the **least popular**?   _____

72. Sally, Mohamed, Dahlia, Peter, and Chris all use various means of transport going to school. Sally and Peter never walk, but sometimes they use their scooters. Sally also occasionally goes by bus, but most of all she prefers to be taken by her mother in the car. Dahlia and Mohamed often use their scooters, but they also cycle or go on foot. Both Chris and Peter ride their bikes most days, but when it rains they catch a bus.

    Who **never** goes on their **bike**?   _____

17

The number codes for three of the four following words are listed randomly below. Work out the **code** to answer the questions.

IDEA   DELI   LIED   DEAL
2563   2537   7256

73.   Find the code for **LIED**.   _____

74.   Find the code for **DALE**.   _____

75.   What does the code **3562** stand for?   _____

76.   What does the code **2733** stand for?   _____

The number codes for three of the four following words are listed randomly below. Work out the **code** to answer the questions.

MATE   TEAR   SEAM   TRAM
2964   5629   3965

77.   Find the code for **SEAM**.   _____

78.   Find the code for **TAME**.   _____

79.   What does the code **3962** stand for?   _____

80.   What does the code **6453** stand for?   _____

TOTAL SCORE: / 80

END OF PRACTICE TEST PAPER 5

PRACTICE TEST PAPER 6

This is a **50 minute test**. Work as quickly, but as accurately, as you can.

Remember: you can also use our _**free self-marking online multiple-choice answer pages**_ that you can use over and over again, plus you'll get an instant test report when you have finished that provides your overall score out of 80.

Simply visit our website here: **https://bit.ly/2SNEHnv** and click on the appropriate button.

In the following, each question uses a different code. Work out the **code** in order to answer the question. Use the alphabet to help you.

Example: _If the code for **CAB** is **GEF**, what is the code for **POTTER**?_   **TSXXIV**

A B C D E F G H I J K L M N O P Q R S T U V W X Y Z

1.   If the code for **CAPITAL** is **DCSMYGS**, what does **DQWXFML** stand for?   _____

2.   If the code for **JACK** is **QZXP**, what is the code for **CALM**?   _____

3.   If the code for **AGAIN** is **WCWEJ**, what does **LKQNO** stand for?   _____

4.   If the code for **LASTS** is **IAPTP**, what is the code for **CUBIC**?   _____

5.   If the code for **WANTS** is **UELXQ**, what is the code for **BORED**?   _____

6.   If the code for **READ** is **IVZW**, what does **YLLI** stand for?   _____

7.   If the code for **HERBAL** is **NKXHGR**, what does **XNESKY** stand for?   _____

In the next questions, the words in the second set follow the same pattern as the words in the first set. Work out the rule to find the **missing word** to complete the second set.

Example: _pour (pod) bud   leaf (?) sit_   **let**

8.   otter (rota) alms   aging (?) elks   _____

9.   rabbit (bite) send   copies (?) atom   _____

10.   folly (loud) used   milks (?) more   _____

11.   abler (beet) suet   igloo (?) slat   _____

19

12. edges (seen) norm   lilac (?) lend   _____

13. Five children visit a bookshop. Jodie spends £15 on two books. Patrick's book costs half as much as Jodie's two. Annis buys a bestseller for 50p more than Patrick's book. Bilal, Noel, and Annis each buy a copy of the same book for £6.

If all these statements are true, only one of the sentences below **must be true**. Which one?

A. Patrick spends the least.   ☐

B. Three children buy two books each.   ☐

C. Only Bilal and Noel share the price of one book.   ☐

D. Patrick's book costs less than Noel's.   ☐

E. Annis spends £14.   ☐

14. Steve, Ronnie, Monty, Claudia, and Liz all enjoy playing video games. Liz dislikes shoot 'em ups, but, like Monty, enjoys platform games. Claudia's favourites are role playing games, but she doesn't play either platform games or shoot 'em ups. Only Ronnie and Steve play F1 games, but all three boys like FIFA games.

If all these statements are true, only one of the sentences below **cannot be true**. Which one?

A. Neither of the girls plays FIFA games.   ☐

B. Neither of the girls enjoys shoot 'em ups.   ☐

C. Ronnie always beats Monty at F1 games.   ☐

D. Steve and Monty are better at platform games than Liz. ☐

E. Claudia is Steve's sister.   ☐

For the questions below, find the **two words** – one from each set – which are the most opposite in meaning.

Example: (funny **happy** sad) (sunken **depressed** bent)

15. (rapid torrent river)   (water stream sluggish)

16. (page read pen)   (write book word)

17. (apostrophe synonym heteronym)   (colon homophone antonym)

18. (dusk dim murky)   (dawn gloomy sun)

19. (dragon hero heroic)   (brave cowardly knight)

In the following, find the **two words** – one from each set – which are the closest in meaning.

Example: (**sound** healthy ill) (**noise** quiet whisper)

20. (pillow bolster blanket)   (feathers down cover)

21. (euphoric euphoria sad)   (ecstatic frown wrinkled)

22. (teach pupil how)   (manners pet train)

23. (man diva tune)   (woman lyric singer)

24. (milk spout jug)   (ewer handle juice)

In the following questions, the numbers in each group are related in the same way. Find the **missing number** in the third group.

Example: 9 (10) 1   4 (7) 3   8 (?) 8   __16__

25. 21 (14) 3   30 (20) 3   16 (?) 4   _____

26. 7 (16) 3   5 (13) 2   9 (?) 5   _____

27. 3 (33) 6   4 (69) 9   8 (?) 2   _____

28. 17 (2) 3   65 (8) 9   48 (?) 13   _____

29. 15 (46) 3   7 (15) 2   6 (?) 5   _____

30. We always stand up when we sing the national **ANM**. _____

31. We all **GD** as Tom calmly removed a scorpion from his arm. _____

32. I usually get a very **STY** nose when I have a cold. _____

33. We need to change the ink **CRIDGE** in the printer. _____

34. As she was so ashamed of him, Mrs Keller **DINED** her son. _____

The number codes for three of the four following words are listed randomly below. Work out the **code** to answer the questions.

REAP   PEER   TRIP   CARP

3824   8964   5684

35. Find the code for **PEER**. _____

36. Find the code for **PART**. _____

37. What does the code **8659** stand for? _____

38. What does the code **5649** stand for? _____

The number codes for three of the four following words are listed randomly below. Work out the **code** to answer the questions.

FLEA   SAFE   CASE   LEAF

8769   3627   9876

39. Find the code for **CASE**. _____

40. Find the code for **LACE**. _____

41. What does the code **9637** stand for? _____

42. What does the code **3688** stand for? _____

Carefully read the following information, then **answer the questions** below.

43. Five children have been invited to Simon's party and they each buy a present for him. Paula spends 70p more than Samantha whose present is half as much as Luigi's. Dina spends £1 less than Luigi. Carlos's present costs twice as much as Paula's. Dina spends £6.

    Who **spends the least**?   _____

44. Max, Samuel, Elizabeth, Fifi, and Gordon were given 20 arithmetic problems. Max got 5 wrong and received 15 marks. Fifi got 2 more marks than Gordon and 1 more than Samuel. Samuel was given 2 more marks than Max, but 1 less than Elizabeth.

    Who received the **lowest mark**?   _____

In the questions below, each letter stands for a number. Work out the **letter solution** to each sum.

Example: $A = 5, B = 3, C = 2, D = 6, E = 11$ $A \times B - C^2 \times C \div E =$ ___C___

45. $A = 9, B = 17, C = 3, D = 12, E = 7$ $A \times C - B + E =$ _____

46. $A = 9, B = 13, C = 15, D = 11, E = 6$ $C - D \times E - B =$ _____

47. $A = 1, B = 2, C = 3, D = 4, E = 5$ $(D^2 - A) \div E =$ _____

48. $A = 12, B = 9, C = 8, D = 3, E = 6$ $E \times A \div C + D =$ _____

49. $A = 1, B = 4, C = 6, D = 7, E = 8$ $(CD + E) - D^2 =$ _____

50. $A = 3, B = 4, C = 5, D = 6$ $(4B + BC) \div D =$ _____

51. $A = 1, B = 2, C = 3, D = 5, E = 7$ $(D^2 - A) \div 4C =$ _____

In each sentence below, a **four-letter word** is hidden at the end of one word and the start of the next. Find the hidden word.

Example: *"I alway<u>s wan</u>ted to be a doctor," Sita said.*   ___*swan*___

52.   "Make sure to remember to wash the spoon," Chef said.   _____

53.   The bucking bronco almost threw the rider off.   _____

54. After the fire, nothing was left but burnt wood and ash. _____

55. The tired man yawned as he sat on the sofa. _____

56. The children had scones for their tea. _____

In the questions below, find the **pair of letters** that most sensibly completes the analogy. Use the alphabet to help you.

Example: **AB** is to **FG** as **QR** is to (UV **VW** WX VU UX).

A B C D E F G H I J K L M N O P Q R S T U V W X Y Z

57. **TG** is to **QJ** as **RI** is to (OL OM OK NL NM).

58. **LO** is to **OL** as **MN** is to (OP PJ PL PK OK).

59. **LP** is to **TM** as **YV** is to (GS FS HR GT FR).

60. **CO** is to **FN** as **JV** is to (NT MU NU MW MV).

61. **EL** is to **OV** as **BD** is to (YW WA VB WY YB).

Three of the words in each of the following lists are related in some way. For each question, find the **two words** which do not belong.

Example: leg arm **heart** hand **lungs**

62. smoke fire flames ash blaze

63. thus hence conversely therefore however

64. slash bang cut bruise lacerate

65. Biro fountain pen pencil stylus quill

66. will future could past present

67. gold silver brass steel lead

68. shield army protect guard navy

In each of the following, find the **two words** – one from the first group and one from the second group – which make a proper new word when combined.

Example: **(bit** *part bite)* *(ton* **ten** *tan)*

69. (on   in   at)   (vest   shirt   top)

70. (see   watch   eye)   (cover   lid   top)

71. (as   so   at)   (noble   king   jack)

72. (breathe   air   flurry) (less   room   gap)

73. (am   are   was)   (hurt   mid   bled)

For each of the following questions, find the **term** that continues the sequence in the most logical way. Use the alphabet to help you.

Example: 2K,   3M,   4O,   5Q,   **6S**

A B C D E F G H I J K L M N O P Q R S T U V W X Y Z

74. rB15, nH13, kJ10, gP6, _____

75. X, Y, A, D, F, G, I, _____

76. IJK, JFM, GBQ, HXS, _____

77. MO, LP, LM, MN, OK, _____

78. D, G, I, J, J, _____

79. 6kC, 5kG, 5lI, 4lM, _____

80. AB, CB, BA, DY, CV, _____

TOTAL SCORE: **/ 80**

END OF PRACTICE TEST PAPER 6

ANSWERS

Pages 26 and 27 provide the answers to Practice Test Papers 4, 5 & 6. The page numbers on the right-hand side of each column indicate where to find each answer's corresponding detailed explanation.

PRACTICE TEST PAPER 4

(1) 6273	p. 28
(2) TIRE	p. 28
(3) AFAR	p. 28
(4) 8426	p. 28
(5) 5826	p. 28
(6) WORE	p. 28
(7) fit; healthy	p. 28
(8) near; approach	p. 28
(9) kind; nice	p. 28
(10) nervous; twitchy	p. 28
(11) king; emperor	p. 28
(12) real; imaginary	p. 28
(13) ancient; youthful	p. 28
(14) breakfast; supper	p. 28
(15) eat; fast	p. 28
(16) rise; descend	p. 29
(17) B	p. 29
(18) E	p. 29
(19) B	p. 29
(20) B	p. 29
(21) D	p. 29
(22) whom	p. 29
(23) rein	p. 29
(24) star	p. 29
(25) pain	p. 29
(26) rage	p. 29
(27) drab	p. 29
(28) ten	p. 29
(29) clue	p. 29
(30) ogre	p. 30
(31) crank	p. 30
(32) hate; mate	p. 30
(33) ride; march	p. 30
(34) paper; book	p. 30
(35) win; receive	p. 30
(36) giant; baby	p. 30
(37) 5	p. 30
(38) 1	p. 30

(39) 3	p. 30
(40) 4	p. 30
(41) 7	p. 31
(42) CORE	p. 31
(43) ORDER	p. 31
(44) BALLET	p. 31
(45) AXPSH	p. 31
(46) WSDTT	p. 31
(47) 40	p. 31
(48) 29	p. 31
(49) 48	p. 31
(50) 15	p. 31
(51) 25	p. 31
(52) torn	p. 31
(53) plod	p. 31
(54) chat	p. 32
(55) nose	p. 32
(56) top	p. 32
(57) pits	p. 32
(58) pour	p. 32
(59) fat; her	p. 32
(60) crumb; led	p. 32
(61) tooth; paste	p. 32
(62) a; side	p. 32
(63) pa; per	p. 32
(64) Stephen	p. 33
(65) Friday	p. 33
(66) 72	p. 33
(67) 49	p. 33
(68) 13	p. 33
(69) 25	p. 33
(70) 6	p. 33
(71) M	p. 33
(72) W	p. 33
(73) L	p. 33
(74) G	p. 33
(75) E	p. 33
(76) QR	p. 33
(77) ON	p. 33
(78) TV	p. 33
(79) IR	p. 33
(80) CX	p. 33

PRACTICE TEST PAPER 5

(1) 14	p. 34
(2) 45	p. 34
(3) 5	p. 34
(4) 43	p. 34
(5) 45	p. 34
(6) 11	p. 34
(7) o	p. 34
(8) z	p. 34
(9) t	p. 34
(10) w	p. 34
(11) r	p. 34
(12) follow; obey	p. 34
(13) mammal; reptile	p. 34
(14) timid; brave	p. 35
(15) tide; emit	p. 35
(16) soul; sail	p. 35
(17) 6	p. 35
(18) 6	p. 35
(19) 7	p. 35
(20) 17	p. 35
(21) 5	p. 35
(22) 4	p. 35
(23) aroma; odour	p. 35
(24) dock; cut	p. 35
(25) volume; tome	p. 35
(26) grateful; thankful	p. 35
(27) organised; orderly	p. 35
(28) nag; mare	p. 36
(29) D	p. 36
(30) E	p. 36
(31) led	p. 36
(32) lunge	p. 36
(33) dram	p. 36
(34) tad	p. 37
(35) just	p. 37
(36) E	p. 37
(37) C	p. 37
(38) C	p. 37
(39) C	p. 37

(40) B   *p. 37*
(41) B   *p. 37*

(42) show; display   *p. 38*
(43) snakes and ladders;   *p. 38*
backgammon
(44) me; she   *p. 38*
(45) sped; rate   *p. 38*
(46) graceful; polished   *p. 38*

(47) jog   *p. 38*
(48) toast   *p. 38*
(49) row   *p. 38*
(50) cast   *p. 38*
(51) mode   *p. 38*
(52) tart   *p. 38*

(53) EP   *p. 38*
(54) FVJ   *p. 38*
(55) H   *p. 38*
(56) 1P   *p. 39*
(57) If10   *p. 39*
(58) KB   *p. 39*
(59) X   *p. 39*

(60) glum   *p. 39*
(61) them   *p. 39*
(62) seen   *p. 39*
(63) scar   *p. 39*
(64) tent   *p. 39*

(65) brief; lengthy   *p. 39*
(66) separate; mix   *p. 39*
(67) apathy; excitement   *p. 39*
(68) insolent; polite   *p. 39*
(69) greedy; generous   *p. 40*
(70) complete; start   *p. 40*

(71) hockey   *p. 40*
(72) Sally   *p. 40*

(73) 3752   *p. 40*
(74) 2635   *p. 40*
(75) LEAD   *p. 40*
(76) DILL   *p. 40*

(77) 3965   *p. 40*
(78) 2659   *p. 40*
(79) SEAT   *p. 40*
(80) ARMS   *p. 40*

PRACTICE TEST PAPER 6

(1) COTTAGE   *p. 41*
(2) XZON   *p. 41*
(3) POURS   *p. 41*
(4) ZUYIZ   *p. 41*
(5) ZSPIB   *p. 41*
(6) BOOR   *p. 41*
(7) RHYMES   *p. 41*

(8) gage   *p. 41*
(9) pest   *p. 41*
(10) lime   *p. 41*
(11) goat   *p. 41*
(12) call   *p. 42*

(13) E   *p. 42*
(14) C   *p. 42*

(15) rapid; sluggish   *p. 42*
(16) read; write   *p. 42*
(17) synonym; antonym   *p. 43*
(18) dusk; dawn   *p. 43*
(19) heroic; cowardly   *p. 43*

(20) blanket; cover   *p. 43*
(21) euphoric; ecstatic   *p. 43*
(22) teach; train   *p. 43*
(23) diva; singer   *p. 43*
(24) jug; ewer   *p. 43*

(25) 8   *p. 43*
(26) 20   *p. 43*
(27) 29   *p. 43*
(28) 5   *p. 43*
(29) 31   *p. 43*

(30) THE   *p. 43*
(31) APE   *p. 43*
(32) NOT   *p. 43*
(33) ART   *p. 43*
(34) SOW   *p. 43*

(35) 4998   *p. 44*
(36) 4683   *p. 44*
(37) RACE   *p. 44*
(38) CAPE   *p. 44*

(39) 3627   *p. 44*
(40) 8637   *p. 44*
(41) FACE   *p. 44*
(42) CALL   *p. 44*

(43) Samantha   *p. 44*
(44) Max   *p. 44*

(45) B   *p. 44*
(46) D   *p. 44*
(47) C   *p. 44*
(48) A   *p. 45*
(49) A   *p. 45*
(50) D   *p. 45*
(51) B   *p. 45*

(52) tore   *p. 45*
(53) coal   *p. 45*
(54) dash   *p. 45*
(55) many   *p. 45*
(56) fort   *p. 45*

(57) OL   *p. 45*
(58) PK   *p. 45*
(59) GS   *p. 45*
(60) MU   *p. 45*
(61) WY   *p. 45*

(62) smoke; ash   *p. 45*
(63) conversely; however   *p. 45*
(64) bang; bruise   *p. 45*
(65) pencil; stylus   *p. 45*
(66) will; could   *p. 45*
(67) brass; steel   *p. 45*
(68) army; navy   *p. 45*

(69) in; vest   *p. 45*
(70) eye; lid   *p. 45*
(71) as; king   *p. 46*
(72) air; less   *p. 46*
(73) am; bled   *p. 46*

(74) dR1   *p. 46*
(75) L   *p. 46*
(76) ETW   *p. 46*
(77) RL   *p. 46*
(78) I   *p. 46*
(79) 4mO   *p. 46*
(80) ER   *p. 47*

PRACTICE TEST PAPER 4: EXPLANATIONS

1. A comparison of the given three numbers and four words reveals that two numbers end with 3 and only two words end with R, **so R = 3**. Hence:
   - The code for FAIR must be either 6523 or 6273
   - The code for FEAR must be either 6523 or 6273
   A further comparison of FAIR and FEAR shows that both words contain the letter A, and that both possible codes contain the digit 2. **By comparing the positions** of the letter A and the number 2, we can deduce that **the code for FAIR must be 6273**.

2. As we know that the code for FAIR is 6273, this means that **the code for FEAR must be 6523**. Therefore: F = 6; A = 2; I = 7; R = 3; E = 5. Since we know that E = 5, 1234 cannot be the code for DARE. Hence, **1234 is the code for DART**. Therefore: D = 1; T = 4. From all this, **by substitution**, we can work out that **the code 4735 stands for TIRE**.

3. As we know all the codes for all the letters, **by substitution**, we can deduce that **the code 2623 stands for AFAR**.

4. A comparison of all four words reveals that two words start with the letter C and the other two words have a second letter C. Similarly, a comparison of all three given numbers reveals that two numbers begin with the digit 4 and the third number has a second digit 4. Therefore: **C = 4**. Consequently:
   - The code for CRAW must be either 4279 or 4289
   - The code for CROW must be either 4279 or 4289
   From this: R = 2; W = 9. Now, as the remaining given number (i.e. 8456) does not contain a 2, this means that **8456 must the code for ACHE** (which is the only word without an R). Therefore: A = 8; H = 5; E = 6. Hence, **by substitution**, we can deduce that **the code for ACRE is 8426**.

5. As we know H = 5; A = 8; R = 2; E = 6, **by substitution**, we can deduce that **the code for HARE is 5826**.

6. As we know that A = 8, this means that **4289 is the code for CRAW** and that **4279 is the code for CROW**. Hence, **O = 7**. Now we have all the codes for all the letters, **by substitution**, we can work out that **9726 is the code for WORE**.

7. The two words closest in meaning in the two given sets are **fit (adj.)** and **healthy (adj.)**.
   - **Fit (adj.)** is being healthy or in good health.
   - **Healthy (adj.)** is being in good health or fit.

8. The two words closest in meaning in the two given sets are **near (v.)** and **approach (v.)**.
   - **Near (v.)** is to come close to, or to approach, something.
   - **Approach (v.)** is to come close to, or near to, something.

9. The two words closest in meaning in the two given sets are **kind (adj.)** and **nice (adj.)**.
   - **Kind (adj.)** is being friendly and generous.
   - **Nice (adj.)** is being friendly and pleasant.

10. The two words closest in meaning in the two given sets are **nervous (adj.)** and **twitchy (adj.)**.
    - **Nervous (adj.)** is being uneasy and anxious.
    - **Twitchy (adj.)** is being anxious or nervous.

11. The two words closest in meaning in the two given sets are **king (n.)** and **emperor (n.)**.
    - **King (n.)** is a male ruler of a kingdom.
    - **Emperor (n.)** is a male ruler of an empire.

12. The two words most opposite in meaning in the two given sets are **real (adj.)** and **imaginary (adj.)**.
    - **Real (adj.)** is being something that actually exists in the world.
    - **Imaginary (adj.)** is being something that is unreal or made up and is to be found only in the mind.

13. The two words most opposite in meaning in the two given sets are **ancient (adj.)** and **youthful (adj.)**.
    - **Ancient (adj.)** is being extremely old.
    - **Youthful (adj.)** is being young or associated with youth.

14. The two words most opposite in meaning in the two given sets are **breakfast (n.)** and **supper (n.)**.
    - **Breakfast (n.)** is the meal that is eaten at the beginning of the day; the first meal of the day.
    - **Supper (n.)** is the meal that is eaten at the end of the day; the last meal of the day.

15. The two words most opposite in meaning in the two given sets are **eat (v.)** and **fast (v.)**.
    - **Eat (v.)** is to consume food.
    - **Fast (v.)** is to not eat or consume food.

16. The two words most opposite in meaning in the two given sets are <u>rise (v.)</u> and <u>descend (v.)</u>.
    - *Rise (v.)* is to move upwards, to ascend, or to elevate.
    - *Descend (v.)* is to move downwards.

17. To see the numerical problem, we substitute the letters for their given values:

    $$B \times E \div C \times D \quad \Rightarrow \quad 24 \times 3 \div 6 \times 2$$

    By carrying out the mathematical operations in stages, we arrive at the numerical answer of the problem:

    $$24 \times 3 = 72 \quad 72 \div 6 = 12 \quad 12 \times 2 = \mathbf{24}$$

    As the number 24 is represented by the letter B, the answer is <u>**B**</u>.

18. To see the numerical problem, we substitute the letters for their given values:

    $$E \div D \times C \div A \quad \Rightarrow \quad 12 \div 6 \times 18 \div 3$$

    By carrying out the mathematical operations in stages, we arrive at the numerical answer of the problem:

    $$12 \div 6 = 2 \quad 2 \times 18 = 36 \quad 36 \div 3 = \mathbf{12}$$

    As the number 12 is represented by the letter E, the answer is <u>**E**</u>.

19. To see the numerical problem, we substitute the letters for their given values:

    $$2C \div (D \div B) \quad \Rightarrow \quad (2 \times 6) \div (12 \div 4)$$

    By carrying out the mathematical operations in stages, we arrive at the numerical answer of the problem:

    $$(2 \times 6) = 12 \quad 12 \div (12 \div 4) = 12 \div (3) \quad 12 \div 3 = \mathbf{4}$$

    As the number 4 is represented by the letter B, the answer is <u>**B**</u>.

20. To see the numerical problem, we substitute the letters for their given values:

    $$(4C + A) \div D \quad \Rightarrow \quad (4 \times 5 + 1) \div 7$$

    By carrying out the mathematical operations in stages, we arrive at the numerical answer of the problem:

    $$(4 \times 5 + 1) = (20 + 1) \quad (20 + 1) = 21 \quad 21 \div 7 = \mathbf{3}$$

    As the number 3 is represented by the letter B, the answer is <u>**B**</u>.

21. To see the numerical problem, we substitute the letters for their given values:

    $$5D \div (A + B) \quad \Rightarrow \quad (5 \times 7) \div (1 + 4)$$

    By carrying out the mathematical operations in stages, we arrive at the numerical answer of the problem:

    $$(5 \times 7) = 35 \quad 35 \div (1 + 4) = 35 \div (5) \quad 35 \div 5 = \mathbf{7}$$

    As the number 7 is represented by the letter D, the answer is <u>**D**</u>.

22. The hidden **four-letter word** is **whom**: The only person <u>who m</u>anaged to solve the problem was Julia.

23. The hidden **four-letter word** is **rein**: "Your glasses a<u>re in</u> their case," Khaled said to his wife.

24. The hidden **four-letter word** is **star**: Toby couldn't recall his la<u>st ar</u>gument.

25. The hidden **four-letter word** is **pain**: "Have you seen Pa<u>pa in</u> his new jacket?" said Mabel.

26. The hidden **four-letter word** is **rage**: We haven't been to the cinema fo<u>r age</u>s.

27. In the first two pairs, the following pattern is used to make the second word of each pair:

    s t a r ⇨ rats   **w a r t s** ⇨ straw
    4 3 2 1   5 4 3 2 1

    The result of applying this pattern to the first word of the third pair is as follows:

    b a r d
    4 3 2 1

    The letters to be used, therefore, are **b, a, r, d** and need to be re-ordered as: **d, r, a, b** = <u>**drab**</u>.

28. In the first two pairs, the following pattern is used to make the second word of each pair:

    i n d i g o ⇨ **din**   **e n d a n g e r** ⇨ **den**
    2 3   1   2 3   1

    The result of applying this pattern to the first word of the third pair is as follows:

    e n t r a n c e
    2 3 1

    The letters to be used, therefore, are **e, n, t** and need to be re-ordered as: **t, e, n** = <u>**ten**</u>.

29. In the first two pairs, the following pattern is used to make the second word of each pair:

bubble ⇨ blue   fumble ⇨ flue
1 3   24   1 3   24

The result of applying this pattern to the first word of the third pair is as follows:

cuddle
1 3   24

The letters to be used, therefore, are **c, u, l, e** and need to be re-ordered as: **c, l, u, e = <u>clue</u>**.

30. In the first two pairs, the following pattern is used to make the second word of each pair:

bale ⇨ able   care ⇨ acre
2 1 3 4   2 1 3 4

The result of applying this pattern to the first word of the third pair is as follows:

gore
2 1 3 4

The letters to be used, therefore, are **g, o, r, e** and need to be re-ordered as: **o, g, r, e = <u>ogre</u>**.

31. In the first two pairs, the following pattern is used to make the second word of each pair:

cheating ⇨ chant   freaking ⇨ frank
1 2   3 5 4   1 2   3 5 4

The result of applying this pattern to the first word of the third pair is as follows:

creaking
1 2   3 5 4

The letters to be used, therefore, are **c, r, a, k, n** and need to be re-ordered as: **c, r, a, n, k = <u>crank</u>**.

32. The analogy common to both pairs is that of **anagrams**. <u>Hate</u> is an anagram of **heat**; <u>mate</u> is an anagram of **meat**.

33. The analogy common to both pairs is that of **actions / verbs associated with a noun**. The members of a **cavalry <u>ride</u>** horses; the members of an **infantry <u>march</u>**.

34. The analogy common to both pairs is that of **parts of compound words**. <u>Paper</u> is the second half of the compound noun **news**paper; <u>book</u> is the second half of the compound noun **note**book.

35. The analogy common to both pairs is that of **actions / verbs associated with a noun**. A **prize** is something that you <u>win</u>; a **gift** is something that you <u>receive</u>.

36. The analogy common to both pairs is that of **movement**. The movement of a <u>giant</u> is described as a **stride**; the movement of a <u>baby</u> is described as a **crawl**.

37. The given equation is as follows: $12 \times 4 - 3 \div 9 = 14 \div 2 + 3 - (?)$. First, solve the left-hand side:
$$12 \times 4 - 3 \div 9 \;=\; 48 - 3 \div 9 \;=\; 45 \div 9 \;=\; \mathbf{5}$$
Then, solve the right-hand side as far as possible:
$$14 \div 2 + 3 - (?) \;=\; 7 + 3 - (?) \;=\; \mathbf{10 - (?)}$$
Put the two sides of the equation together: $\mathbf{5 = 10 - (?)}$. The missing number is, therefore, **<u>5</u>**.

38. The given equation is as follows: $6 + 5 - 3 \times 4 = 11 \times 2 + 9 + (?)$. First, solve the left-hand side:
$$6 + 5 - 3 \times 4 \;=\; 11 - 3 \times 4 \;=\; 8 \times 4 \;=\; \mathbf{32}$$
Then, solve the right-hand side as far as possible:
$$11 \times 2 + 9 + (?) \;=\; 22 + 9 + (?) \;=\; \mathbf{31 + (?)}$$
Put the two sides of the equation together: $\mathbf{32 = 31 + (?)}$. The missing number is, therefore, **<u>1</u>**.

39. The given equation is as follows: $16 - 5 \times 4 = 17 \times 3 - 10 + (?)$. First, solve the left-hand side:
$$16 - 5 \times 4 \;=\; 11 \times 4 \;=\; \mathbf{44}$$
Then, solve the right-hand side as far as possible:
$$17 \times 3 - 10 + (?) \;=\; 51 - 10 + (?) \;=\; \mathbf{41 + (?)}$$
Put the two sides of the equation together: $\mathbf{44 = 41 + (?)}$. The missing number is, therefore, **<u>3</u>**.

40. The given equation is as follows: $64 \div 8 + 5 = 3 \times 15 \div 5 + (?)$. First, solve the left-hand side:
$$64 \div 8 + 5 \;=\; 8 + 5 \;=\; \mathbf{13}$$
Then, solve the right-hand side as far as possible:
$$3 \times 15 \div 5 + (?) \;=\; 45 \div 5 + (?) \;=\; \mathbf{9 + (?)}$$
Put the two sides of the equation together: $\mathbf{13 = 9 + (?)}$. The missing number is, therefore, **<u>4</u>**.

41. The given equation is as follows: $39 - 6 \div 11 = 26 - 5 \div (?)$. First, solve the left-hand side:

$$39 - 6 \div 11 = 33 \div 11 = 3$$

Then, solve the right-hand side as far as possible:

$$26 - 5 \div (?) = 21 \div (?)$$

Put the two sides of the equation together: $3 = 21 \div (?)$. The missing number is, therefore, **7**.

42. This is a **mirror code** where each letter and its code are equal distances from the middle of the alphabet (i.e. the space between M and N). Hence, the word that the code XLIV stands for is found in the following way: **the mirror reflection of X = C; the mirror reflection of L = O; the mirror reflection of I = R; the mirror reflection of V = E.** The word that the code **XLIV** stands for is, therefore, **CORE**.

43. This is a **complex code** which is obtained by moving the letters of the word using the sequence $-2, +4, -2, +4, -2$. Hence, to de-code MVBIP, the encoding pattern is reversed in the following way: **M + 2 places = O; V − 4 places = R; B + 2 places = D; I − 4 places = E; P + 2 places = R.** The code **MVBIP**, therefore, stands for the word **ORDER**.

44. This is a **simple code** where each letter and its code are as follows: T is encoded as Y; A is encoded as D; B is encoded as J; L is encoded as R; E is encoded as V. Hence, the word that the code JDRRVY stands for is found in the following way: **J is the code for B; D is the code for A; R is the code for L; R is the code for L; Y is the code for T.** The word that the code **JDRRVY** stands for is, therefore, **BALLET**.

45. This is a **complex code** which is obtained by moving the letters of the word using the sequence $-4, -3, -2, -1, -0$. Hence, the code for EARTH is found in the following way: **E − 4 places = A; A − 3 places = X; R − 2 places = P; T − 1 place = S; H − 0 places = H.** The code for **EARTH** is, therefore, **AXPSH**.

46. This is a **complex code** which is obtained by moving the letters of the word using the sequence $+5, +4, +3, +2, +1$. Hence, the code for ROARS is found in the following way: **R + 5 places = W; O + 4 places = S; A + 3 places = D; R + 2 places = T; S + 1 place = T.** The code for **ROARS** is, therefore, **WSDTT**.

47. This number sequence is formed by **following the pattern − 2, − 3, − 4 to obtain the next term**:

$$54 \, (-2=) \, 52 \, (-3=) \, 49 \, (-4=) \, 45$$

According to this pattern, the next term in this sequence is $45 \, (-5=)$ **40**.

48. This number sequence is formed by **adding each two consecutive terms together to obtain the next one**:

$$3 \, (+) \, 4 \, (=) \, 7 \, (+4=) \, 11 \, (+7=) \, 18$$

According to this pattern, the next term in this sequence is **18 (+ 11 =)** **29**.

49. This number sequence is formed by **multiplying the number 12 by even numbers in descending order, starting with 12, to obtain the next term**:

$$(12 \times 12 =) \, 144 \, (12 \times 10 =) \, 120 \, (12 \times 8 =) \, 96 \, (12 \times 6 =) \, 72$$

According to this pattern, the next term in this sequence is $(12 \times 4 =)$ **48**.

50. This number sequence is formed of **two alternating series**. In the first series: <u>3</u>, 6, <u>7</u>, 5, <u>11</u>, 4, the next term is obtained by **adding 4**:

$$3 \, (+4=) \, 7 \, (+4=) \, 11$$

In the second series: 3, <u>6</u>, 7, <u>5</u>, 11, <u>4</u>, the next term is obtained by **subtracting 1**:

$$6 \, (-1=) \, 5 \, (-1=) \, 4$$

As the next term in the sequence belongs to the first series, the term will be $11 \, (+4=)$ **15**.

51. This number sequence is formed by **following the pattern + 3, + 5, + 7 to obtain the next term**:

$$1 \, (+3=) \, 4 \, (+5=) \, 9 \, (+7=) \, 16$$

According to this pattern, the next term in this sequence is $16 \, (+9=)$ **25**.

52. The first set of words is governed by the following rule:

h a p p y (p a r t) s o r t
  2 1   1 2 3 4   3 4

By applying this rule to the second set of words we can see the following:

p o r t s (?) b a r n
  2 1   3 4

The letters to be used, therefore, are **o, t, r, n** and need to be re-ordered as: **t, o, r, n = torn**.

53. The first set of words is governed by the following rule:

i t e m (m i l e) l e f t
2 1   1 23 4 3 4

By applying this rule to the second set of words we can see the following:

l e a <u>p</u> (?) <u>o</u> <u>d</u> e s
   2   1   3 4

The letters to be used, therefore, are **l, p, o, d** and need to be re-ordered as: **p, l, o, d = <u>plod</u>**.

54. The first set of words is governed by the following rule:

m a <u>ll</u> (t e l l) r a <u>t</u> <u>e</u>
    3 4 1 2 3 4   1 2

By applying this rule to the second set of words we can see the following:

b e <u>a</u> <u>t</u> (?) m u <u>c</u> h
   3 4   1 2

The letters to be used, therefore, are **a, t, c, h** and need to be re-ordered as: **c, h, a, t = <u>chat</u>**.

55. The first set of words is governed by the following rule:

e a r <u>l</u> (l o f t) <u>f</u> <u>o</u> o t
     1 1 2 3 4 3 2 4

By applying this rule to the second set of words we can see the following:

o p e <u>n</u> (?) <u>s</u> <u>o</u> r e
     1   3 2 4

The letters to be used, therefore, are **n, s, o, e** and need to be re-ordered as: **n, o, s, e = <u>nose</u>**.

56. The first set of words is governed by the following rule:

s <u>l</u> i m (l o w) <u>w</u> <u>o</u> o d
  1   1 2 3 3 2

By applying this rule to the second set of words we can see the following:

s <u>t</u> e p (?) <u>p</u> <u>o</u> l l
  1   3 2

The letters to be used, therefore, are **t, p, o** and need to be re-ordered as: **t, o p = <u>top</u>**.

57. The first set of words is governed by the following rule:

p <u>a</u> <u>s</u> s (l a s t) <u>t</u> o o <u>l</u>
  2 3   1 2 3 4 4   1

By applying this rule to the second set of words we can see the following:

w <u>i</u> <u>t</u> h (?) <u>s</u> o u <u>p</u>
  2 3   4   1

The letters to be used, therefore, are **i, t, s, p** and need to be re-ordered as: **p, i, t, s = <u>pits</u>**.

58. The first set of words is governed by the following rule:

s <u>c</u> <u>o</u> r e (c o a l) <u>a</u> <u>l</u> l
  1 2   1 2 3 4 3 4

By applying this rule to the second set of words we can see the following:

s <u>p</u> <u>o</u> r t (?) <u>u</u> <u>r</u> n
  1 2   3 4

The letters to be used, therefore, are **p, o, u, r** and are to be kept in this order – i.e. **<u>pour</u>**.

59. The only two words that form a proper word when combined are <u>**fat**</u> and <u>**her**</u> to give **father**. No other combinations are proper, or incorrectly spelled, words.

60. The only two words that form a proper word when combined are <u>**crumb**</u> and <u>**led**</u> to give **crumbled**. No other combinations are proper, or incorrectly spelled, words.

61. The only two words that form a proper word when combined are <u>**tooth**</u> and <u>**paste**</u> to give **toothpaste**. No other combinations are proper, or incorrectly spelled, words.

62. The only two words that form a proper word when combined are <u>**a**</u> and <u>**side**</u> to give **aside**. Aline (a + line) is an incorrect spelling of 'align'; atack (a + tack) is an incorrect spelling of 'attack'; asside (as + side) is an incorrect spelling of 'aside'.

63. The only two words that form a proper word when combined are <u>**pa**</u> and <u>**per**</u> to give **paper**. Papar (pa + par) is an

incorrect spelling of either 'paper' or 'papa'; granpar (gran + par) is an incorrect spelling of 'grandpa'.

64. Using the information given, we can deduce that each child received the following presents, and, that of all the children, <u>**Stephen**</u> **received the most presents** *(viz. 3)*:

John	Harry	Alan	Mark	Stephen
Football			Football	
	DVD		DVD	DVD
Video game	Video game	Video game	~~Video game~~	Video game
		Book		Book

65. Using the information given, we can deduce which days each child can attend the party, and, that of all the days, <u>**Friday**</u> **is the day when most children can attend** *(viz. 4)*:

Greg	Simon	Harry	David	Boris
Monday			Monday	
	Tuesday	Tuesday	Tuesday	
	Wednesday	Wednesday		Wednesday
Thursday	Thursday	Thursday		
	Friday	Friday	Friday	Friday

66. Each time, the first number is multiplied by the third number; then the product is multiplied by 2 to get the second number:
11 (66) 3 ⇨ 11 x 3 = 33; 33 x 2 = 66 ● 12 (96) 4 ⇨ 12 x 4 = 48; 48 x 2 = 96 ● **9 (?) 4 ⇨ 9 x 4 = 36; 36 x 2 = <u>72</u>**

67. Each time, the third number is subtracted from the first number; then the result is squared to get the second number:
11 (64) 3 ⇨ 11 − 3 = 8; 8 x 8 = 64 ● 7 (4) 5 ⇨ 7 − 5 = 2; 2 x 2 = 4 ● **9 (?) 2 ⇨ 9 − 2 = 7; 7 x 7 = <u>49</u>**

68. Each time, the third number is subtracted from the first number; then 4 is added to the result to get the second number:
26 (15) 15 ⇨ 26 − 15 = 11; 11 + 4 = 15 ● 42 (34) 12 ⇨ 42 − 12 = 30; 30 + 4 = 34 ● **20 (?) 11 ⇨ 20 − 11 = 9; 9 + 4 = <u>13</u>**

69. Each time, the first and third numbers are squared; then their products are added together to get the second number:
3 (13) 2 ⇨ 3 x 3 = 9; 2 x 2 = 4; 9 + 4 = 13 ● 5 (34) 3 ⇨ 5 x 5 = 25; 3 x 3 = 9; 25 + 9 = 34 ●
4 (?) 3 ⇨ 4 x 4 = 16; 3 x 3 = 9; 16 + 9 = <u>25</u>

70. Each time, the third number is divided by the first number; then 3 is subtracted from the result to get the second number:
7 (4) 49 ⇨ 49 ÷ 7 = 7; 7 − 3 = 4 ● 3 (11) 42 ⇨ 42 ÷ 3 = 14; 14 − 3 = 11 ● **6 (?) 54 ⇨ 54 ÷ 6 = 9; 9 − 3 = <u>6</u>**

71. By removing <u>**M**</u> from BOMB and adding it to RAP, we get the new words: **BOB   RA<u>M</u>P**. No other letters can be removed from BOMB to give a proper word.

72. By removing <u>**W**</u> from O<u>W</u>N and adding it to SADDLE, we get the new words: **ON   S<u>W</u>ADDLE**. While N can be removed from OWN to give OW, it cannot be added to SADDLE in any way to form a proper word.

73. By removing <u>L</u> from CUL T and adding it to BET, we get the new words: **CUT   BE<u>L</u>T**. No other letters can be removed from CULT to give a proper word.

74. By removing <u>**G**</u> from <u>G</u>RID and adding it to REIN, we get the new words: **RID   REI<u>G</u>N**. While R can be removed from GRID to give GID, it cannot be added to REIN in any way to form a proper word.

75. By removing <u>**E**</u> from L<u>E</u>AST and adding it to HOP, we get the new words: **LAST   HOP<u>E</u>**. While the letters L, A, and T can be removed from LEAST to give EAST, LEST, and LEAS respectively, neither the L, A, nor the T can be added to HOP in any way to form a proper word.

76. To find the missing letter pair, **M moves + 4 places to Q** and **X moves − 6 places to R** ⇨ **<u>QR</u>**.

77. To find the missing letter pair, **L is mirrored to obtain O** and **M is mirrored to obtain N** ⇨ **<u>ON</u>**.

78. To find the missing letter pair, **T moves + 0 places to T** and **U moves + 1 place to V** ⇨ **<u>TV</u>**.

79. To find the missing letter pair, **EV is a mirror pair (E is the mirror of V); E moves + 4 places to I; I is then mirrored to obtain R** ⇨ **<u>IR</u>**.

80. To find the missing letter pair, **V moves + 7 places to C** and **C moves − 5 places to X** ⇨ **<u>CX</u>**.

PRACTICE TEST PAPER 5: EXPLANATIONS

1. This number sequence is formed of **two alternating series**. In the first series: <u>3</u>, 8, <u>6</u>, 11, <u>9</u>, the next term is obtained by **adding 3 each time**:

   $$3 (+ 3 =) 6 (+ 3 =) 9$$

   In the second series: 3, <u>8</u>, 6, <u>11</u>, 9, the next term is also obtained by **adding 3 each time**:

   $$8 (+ 3 =) 11$$

   As the next term in the sequence belongs to the second series, the term will be 11 (+ 3 =) **14**.

2. This number sequence is formed of **two alternating series**. In the first series: <u>39</u>, 41, <u>38</u>, 43, <u>37</u>, the next term is obtained by **subtracting 1 each time**:

   $$39 (- 1 =) 38 (- 1 =) 37$$

   In the second series: 39, <u>41</u>, 38, <u>43</u>, 37, the next term is obtained by **adding 2 each time**:

   $$41 (+ 2 =) 43$$

   As the next term in the sequence belongs to the second series, the term will be 43 (+ 2 =) **45**.

3. This number sequence is formed of **two alternating series**. In the first series: <u>2</u>, 1, <u>3</u>, 3, <u>4</u>, 5, the next term is obtained by **adding 1 each time**:

   $$2 (+ 1 =) 3 (+ 1 =) 4$$

   In the second series: 2, <u>1</u>, 3, <u>3</u>, 4, <u>5</u>, the next term is obtained by **adding 2 each time**:

   $$1 (+ 2 =) 3 (+ 2 =) 5$$

   As the next term in the sequence belongs to the first series, the term will be 4 (+ 1 =) **5**.

4. This number sequence is formed of **two alternating series**. In the first series: <u>49</u>, 37, <u>47</u>, 39, <u>45</u>, 41, the next term is obtained by **subtracting 2 each time**:

   $$49 (- 2 =) 47 (- 2 =) 45$$

   In the second series: 49, <u>37</u>, 47, <u>39</u>, 45, <u>41</u>, the next term is obtained by **adding 2 each time**:

   $$37 (+ 2 =) 39 (+ 2 =) 41$$

   As the next term in the sequence belongs to the first series, the term will be 45 (- 2 =) **43**.

5. This number sequence is formed by **adding each two consecutive terms together to obtain the next one**:

   $$5 (+) 6 (=) 11 (+ 6 =) 17 (+ 11 =) 28$$

   According to this pattern, the next term in this sequence is 28 (+ 17 =) **45**.

6. This number sequence is formed of **two alternating series**. In the first series: <u>5</u>, 1, <u>10</u>, 6, <u>15</u>, the next term is obtained by **adding 5 each time**:

   $$5 (+ 5 =) 10 (+ 5 =) 15$$

   In the second series: 5, <u>1</u>, 10, <u>6</u>, 15, the next term is also obtained by **adding 5 each time**:

   $$1 (+ 5 =) 6$$

   As the next term in the sequence belongs to the second series, the term will be 6 (+ 5 =) **11**.

7. Adding <u>**o**</u> to the given letter clusters results in the following words: **her<u>o</u>   <u>o</u>men   hell<u>o</u>   <u>o</u>ats**. The letters a, b, c, d, e, f, h, m, p, r, s, t, and v can be used to complete some, but not all four, of the letter clusters.

8. Adding <u>**z**</u> to the given letter clusters results in the following words: **whizz   zone   buzz   zany**. The letters b, c, d, g, h, l, m, n, and t can be used to complete some, but not all four, of the letter clusters.

9. Adding <u>**t**</u> to the given letter clusters results in the following words: **dent   tend   tent   task**. The letters b, c, d, f, l, m, p, r, s, v, and w can be used to complete some, but not all four, of the letter clusters.

10. Adding <u>**w**</u> to the given letter clusters results in the following words: **draw   where   claw   will**. The letters b, d, f, g, h, k, m, n, p, r, s, t, and y can be used to complete some, but not all four, of the letter clusters.

11. Adding <u>**r**</u> to the given letter clusters results in the following words: **your   rice   piper   rink**. The letters d, k, l, m, n, o, p, s, v, and w can be used to complete some, but not all four, of the letter clusters.

12. The analogy common to both pairs is that of **antonyms**. <u>**Follow**</u> is the opposite of **lead**; <u>**obey**</u> is the opposite of **order**.

13. The analogy common to both pairs is that of **types of creatures**. A **whale** is a <u>**mammal**</u>; a **snake** is a <u>**reptile**</u>.

34

14.	The analogy common to both pairs is that of **adjectives/qualities associated with nouns**. A **coward** is <u>timid</u>; a **hero** is <u>brave</u>.
15.	The analogy common to both pairs is that of **word reflections**. **Edit** is the reflection of <u>tide</u>; **time** is the reflection of <u>emit</u>.
16.	The analogy common to both pairs is that of **homophones**. **Sole** is the homophone of <u>soul</u>; **sale** is the homophone of <u>sail</u>.
17.	The given equation is as follows: $41 \times 2 - 1 \div 9 = 7 \times 6 + 12 \div (\,?\,)$. First, solve the left-hand side: $$41 \times 2 - 1 \div 9 = 82 - 1 \div 9 = 81 \div 9 = 9$$ Then, solve the right-hand side as far as possible: $$7 \times 6 + 12 \div (\,?\,) = 42 + 12 \div (\,?\,) = \mathbf{54 \div (\,?\,)}$$ Put the two sides of the equation together: $\mathbf{9 = 54 \div (\,?\,)}$. The missing number is, therefore, <u>**6**</u>.
18.	The given equation is as follows: $23 - 7 \times 2 \div 4 = 15 \div 5 + 11 - (\,?\,)$. First, solve the left-hand side: $$23 - 7 \times 2 \div 4 = 16 \times 2 \div 4 = 32 \div 4 = 8$$ Then, solve the right-hand side as far as possible: $$15 \div 5 + 11 - (\,?\,) = 3 + 11 - (\,?\,) = \mathbf{14 - (\,?\,)}$$ Put the two sides of the equation together: $\mathbf{8 = 14 - (\,?\,)}$. The missing number is, therefore, <u>**6**</u>.
19.	The given equation is as follows: $28 + 8 \div 12 = 63 \div 3 \div (\,?\,)$. First, solve the left-hand side: $$28 + 8 \div 12 = 36 \div 12 = 3$$ Then, solve the right-hand side as far as possible: $$63 \div 3 \div (\,?\,) = \mathbf{21 \div (\,?\,)}$$ Put the two sides of the equation together: $\mathbf{3 = 21 \div (\,?\,)}$. The missing number is, therefore, <u>**7**</u>.
20.	The given equation is as follows: $64 \div 8 \times 3 - 1 = 9 \div 3 \times 2 + (\,?\,)$. First, solve the left-hand side: $$64 \div 8 \times 3 - 1 = 8 \times 3 - 1 = 24 - 1 = 23$$ Then, solve the right-hand side as far as possible: $$9 \div 3 \times 2 + (\,?\,) = 3 \times 2 + (\,?\,) = \mathbf{6 + (\,?\,)}$$ Put the two sides of the equation together: $\mathbf{23 = 6 + (\,?\,)}$. The missing number is, therefore, <u>**17**</u>.
21.	The given equation is as follows: $34 - 4 \div 6 = 75 \div 3 - 15 - (\,?\,)$. First, solve the left-hand side: $$34 - 4 \div 6 = 30 \div 6 = 5$$ Then, solve the right-hand side as far as possible: $$75 \div 3 - 15 - (\,?\,) = 25 - 15 - (\,?\,) = \mathbf{10 - (\,?\,)}$$ Put the two sides of the equation together: $\mathbf{5 = 10 - (\,?\,)}$. The missing number is, therefore, <u>**5**</u>.
22.	The given equation is as follows: $72 \div 9 \times 2 - 1 = 25 + 8 \div 3 + (\,?\,)$. First, solve the left-hand side: $$72 \div 9 \times 2 - 1 = 8 \times 2 - 1 = 16 - 1 = 15$$ Then, solve the right-hand side as far as possible: $$25 + 8 \div 3 + (\,?\,) = 33 \div 3 + (\,?\,) = \mathbf{11 + (\,?\,)}$$ Put the two sides of the equation together: $\mathbf{15 = 11 + (\,?\,)}$. The missing number is, therefore, <u>**4**</u>.
23.	The two words closest in meaning in the two given sets are <u>**aroma (n.)**</u> and <u>**odour (n.)**</u>. • *Aroma (n.) is* a smell. • *Odour (n.) is* a smell.
24.	The two words closest in meaning in the two given sets are <u>**dock (v.)**</u> and <u>**cut (v.)**</u>. • *Dock (v.) is* to cut the end off something, or to remove something entirely (often the tail of an animal). • *Cut (v.) is* to sever one thing from another using a sharp instrument like a knife or a pair of scissors etc.
25.	The two words closest in meaning in the two given sets are <u>**volume (n.)**</u> and <u>**tome (n.)**</u>. • *Volume (n.) is* a book, usually a large or heavy one. • *Tome (n.) is* a book, usually a large or heavy one.
26.	The two words closest in meaning in the two given sets are <u>**grateful (adj.)**</u> and <u>**thankful (adj.)**</u>. • *Grateful (adj.) is* feeling thankful. • *Thankful (adj.) is* feeling grateful.
27.	The two words closest in meaning in the two given sets are <u>**organised (adj.)**</u> and <u>**orderly (adj.)**</u>. • *Organised (adj.) is* having a structure or an order; being well-arranged. • *Orderly (adj.) is* being well-arranged; placed in order or having a structure.

28. The two words closest in meaning in the two given sets are **nag (n.)** and **mare (n.)**.
- *Nag (n.) is* an adult horse that is usually old and run-down.
- *Mare (n.) is* an adult female horse.

29. Using the information given, we can deduce which fish are eaten by each child:

Plaice	Halibut	Cod	Salmon	Tuna
Sally	Sally	Sally	Sally	
Maurice	Maurice		~~Maurice~~	
		~~John~~	~~John~~	John
		~~Mary~~	~~Mary~~	Mary
				Michael

Therefore:

A. Three of them never eat salmon ⇨ is true. Maurice, Mary, and John never eat salmon.

B. Cod is the least popular ⇨ might be true. John and Mary never eat cod and <u>Maurice only likes plaice</u> and halibut.

C. Mary eats halibut ⇨ might be true. We are told that she likes tuna, but we are not told what other fish she likes eating.

D. Maurice and John both like tuna ⇨ **<u>cannot be true</u>. We are told that Maurice only likes plaice and halibut.**

E. Sally likes at least three kinds of fish ⇨ is true. Sally enjoys four kinds of fish: plaice, halibut, cod, and salmon.

30. Using the information given, we can deduce that each of the children received the following number of votes:

David	Petra	Andy	Lindsay	Molly
5 votes	5 votes	5 votes	6 votes	10 votes
			$(10 - 4)$	$(5 + 5)$

Therefore:

A. Molly received eleven votes ⇨ is not true. We are told that Molly received five more votes than Andy, and that Andy received five votes. Therefore, Molly received ten votes, not eleven.

B. David got six fewer votes than Molly ⇨ is not true. Molly got ten votes and David got five votes. Therefore, David received 5 fewer votes than Molly.

C. There were thirty-four children in the class ⇨ might be true. We are not told how many children were in the class.

D. David and Andy were friends ⇨ might be true. We do not know whether they were friends or not.

E. Lindsay received six votes ⇨ **<u>must be true</u>. Since Molly received ten votes and Lindsay got four fewer than Molly, Lindsay received six votes.**

31. In the first two pairs, the following pattern is used to make the second word of each pair:

a b s o r b e d ⇨ **bed**
   1   2 3

o f f e r e d ⇨ **fed**
   1   2 3

The result of applying this pattern to the first word of the third pair is as follows:

a l i g n e d
   1   2 3

The letters to be used, therefore, are **l, e, d** and are to be kept in this order – i.e. **<u>led</u>**.

32. In the first two pairs, the following pattern is used to make the second word of each pair:

d e r i v e d ⇨ **drive**
1   2 3 4 5

c o u r s e d ⇨ **curse**
1   2 3 4 5

The result of applying this pattern to the first word of the third pair is as follows:

l o u n g e d
1   2 3 4 5

The letters to be used, therefore, are **l, u, n, g, e** and are to be kept in this order – i.e. **<u>lunge</u>**.

33. In the first two pairs, the following pattern is used to make the second word of each pair:

t r a m p ⇨ **part**
4 3 2 1

p o r t e d ⇨ **drop**
4 3 2 1

The result of applying this pattern to the first word of the third pair is as follows:

m a r r i e d
4 3 2   1

The letters to be used, therefore, are **m, a, r, d** and need to be re-ordered as: **d, r, a, m = <u>dram</u>**.

34. In the first two pairs, the following pattern is used to make the second word of each pair:

b r e a d e d ⇨ **bad**   **s p e a r e d** ⇨ **sad**
1   2   3   1   2   3

The result of applying this pattern to the first word of the third pair is as follows:

t r e a t e d
1   2   3

The letters to be used, therefore, are **t, a, d** and are to be kept in this order – i.e. **<u>tad</u>**.

35. In the first two pairs, the following pattern is used to make the second word of each pair:

c o u r t e d ⇨ **curt**   **f o u n d e d** ⇨ **fund**
1   2 3 4   1   2 3 4

The result of applying this pattern to the first word of the third pair is as follows:

j o u s t e d
1   2 3 4

The letters to be used, therefore, are **j, u, s, t** and are to be kept in this order – i.e. **<u>just</u>**.

36. To see the numerical problem, we substitute the letters for their given values:

$$D + B - C - A \quad ⇨ \quad 25 + 5 - 13 - 7$$

By carrying out the mathematical operations in stages, we arrive at the numerical answer of the problem:

$$25 + 5 = 30 \quad 30 - 13 = 17 \quad 17 - 7 = \mathbf{10}$$

As the number 10 is represented by the letter E, the answer is **<u>E</u>**.

37. To see the numerical problem, we substitute the letters for their given values:

$$(ED - B) \div AC \quad ⇨ \quad (9 \times 6 - 4) \div (2 \times 5)$$

By carrying out the mathematical operations in stages, we arrive at the numerical answer of the problem:

$$(9 \times 6 - 4) = (54 - 4) \quad 54 - 4 = 50 \quad 50 \div (2 \times 5) = 50 \div (10) \quad 50 \div 10 = \mathbf{5}$$

As the number 5 is represented by the letter C, the answer is **<u>C</u>**.

38. To see the numerical problem, we substitute the letters for their given values:

$$A \div B + E - D \quad ⇨ \quad 8 \div 2 + 15 - 6$$

By carrying out the mathematical operations in stages, we arrive at the numerical answer of the problem:

$$8 \div 2 = 4 \quad 4 + 15 = 19 \quad 19 - 6 = \mathbf{13}$$

As the number 13 is represented by the letter C, the answer is **<u>C</u>**.

39. To see the numerical problem, we substitute the letters for their given values:

$$(AB + AD) \div C \quad ⇨ \quad (3 \times 4 + 3 \times 8) \div 6$$

By carrying out the mathematical operations in stages, we arrive at the numerical answer of the problem:

$$(3 \times 4 + 3 \times 8) = (12 + 3 \times 8) \quad (12 + 3 \times 8) = (12 + 24) \quad (12 + 24) = 36 \quad 36 \div 6 = \mathbf{6}$$

As the number 6 is represented by the letter C, the answer is **<u>C</u>**.

40. To see the numerical problem, we substitute the letters for their given values:

$$A - E \times D - B \quad ⇨ \quad 25 - 20 \times 12 - 30$$

By carrying out the mathematical operations in stages, we arrive at the numerical answer of the problem:

$$25 - 20 = 5 \quad 5 \times 12 = 60 \quad 60 - 30 = \mathbf{30}$$

As the number 30 is represented by the letter B, the answer is **<u>B</u>**.

41. To see the numerical problem, we substitute the letters for their given values:

$$(C^2 + B) \div (A + D) \quad ⇨ \quad (6^2 + 4) \div (3 + 7)$$

By carrying out the mathematical operations in stages, we arrive at the numerical answer of the problem:

$$(6^2 + 4) = (36 + 4) \quad (36 + 4) = 40 \quad 40 \div (3 + 7) = 40 \div (10) \quad 40 \div 10 = \mathbf{4}$$

As the number 4 is represented by the letter B, the answer is **<u>B</u>**.

42. <u>Show</u> and <u>display</u> are the odd ones out because they **are synonymous verbs meaning to exhibit or demonstrate**, whereas study, examine, and inspect are synonymous verbs meaning to look at carefully.

43. <u>Snakes and ladders</u> and <u>backgammon</u> are the odd ones out because they **are games which use dice**, whereas chess, Scrabble, and draughts are all games that do not use dice.

44. <u>Me</u> and <u>she</u> are the odd ones out because they **are pronouns**, whereas a, the, and an are determiners.

45. <u>Sped</u> and <u>rate</u> are the odd ones out because **sped is a verb in the past tense and rate is both a noun and a verb**, whereas quickly, slowly, and hastily are adverbs.

46. <u>Graceful</u> and <u>polished</u> are the odd ones out because they **are adjectives**, whereas elegance, grace, and refinement are nouns.

47. The one word from the list that relates to both groups of words is <u>jog</u>.
    - *Jog (v.)* is to run at a regular speed or pace, often as a form of exercise *(i.e. 'run'; 'trot' - 1st group)*.
    - *Jog (v.)* is to remind someone of something *(i.e. 'nudge'; 'prod' - 2nd group)*.

48. The one word from the list that relates to both groups of words is <u>toast</u>.
    - *Toast (v.)* is to make something brown in colour (usually by cooking it) by exposing the thing to heat directly *(i.e. 'grill'; 'brown' - 1st group)*.
    - *Toast (v.)* is to have a drink in honour of someone or something, or in celebration of someone or something *(i.e. 'honour'; 'salute' - 2nd group)*.

49. The one word from the list that relates to both groups of words is <u>row</u>.
    - *Row (n.)* is a group of things that have been arranged in a line *(i.e. 'line'; 'tier' - 1st group)*.
    - *Row (n.)* is an argument, usually one that is quite loud and angry *(i.e. 'quarrel'; 'argument' - 2nd group)*.

50. The one word from the list that relates to both groups of words is <u>cast</u>.
    - *Cast (n.)* is a collective noun for a group of people performing in a play, film, etc. *(i.e. 'actors'; 'company' - 1st group)*.
    - *Cast (v.)* is to throw something *(i.e. 'throw'; 'hurl' - 2nd group)*.

51. The one word from the list that relates to both groups of words is <u>mode</u>.
    - *Mode (n.)* is a style or fashion, e.g. in clothing, art, etc. *(i.e. 'fashion'; 'vogue' - 1st group)*.
    - *Mode (n.)* is the means by which something is done or happens *(i.e. 'method'; 'way' - 2nd group)*.

52. The one word from the list that relates to both groups of words is <u>tart</u>.
    - *Tart (n.)* is something that is eaten that is made of a pastry case and a filling that can be sweet or savoury *(i.e. 'pie'; 'pastry' - 1st group)*.
    - *Tart (adj.)* is having a taste that is sour or sharp *(i.e. 'sour'; 'bitter' - 2nd group)*.

53. Each term in this letter sequence consists of two capital letters. The first capital letter in each term **moves − 3 places every time**:

    $$T (− 3 =) Q (− 3 =) N (− 3 =) K (− 3 =) H$$

    Hence, the first capital letter of the next term of the sequence is **H (− 3 =) <u>E</u>**. The second capital letter in each term **moves + 3 places every time**:

    $$A (+ 3 =) D (+ 3 =) G (+ 3 =) J (+ 3 =) M$$

    Hence, the second capital letter of the next term of the sequence is **M (+ 3 =) <u>P</u>**. Thus, the next complete term of this sequence is <u>EP</u>.

54. Each term in this letter sequence consists of three capital letters. The first capital letter in each term **moves + 1 place every time**:

    $$B (+ 1 =) C (+ 1 =) D (+ 1 =) E$$

    Hence, the first capital letter of the next term of the sequence is **E (+ 1 =) <u>F</u>**. The second capital letter in each term **moves − 2 places every time**:

    $$D (− 2 =) B (− 2 =) Z (− 2 =) X$$

    Hence, the second capital letter of the next term of the sequence is **X (− 2 =) <u>V</u>**. The third capital letter in each term **moves + 1 place every time**:

    $$F (+ 1 =) G (+ 1 =) H (+ 1 =) I$$

    Hence, the third capital letter of the next term of the sequence is **I (+ 1 =) <u>J</u>**. Thus, the next complete term of this sequence is <u>FVJ</u>.

55. Each term in this sequence is formed of a single capital letter. Each time, the capital letter **moves according to the pattern − 1, − 2, − 3, − 4**:

    $$W (− 1 =) V (− 2 =) T (− 3 =) Q (− 4 =) M$$

    Hence, the capital letter of the next term of the sequence is **M (− 5 =) <u>H</u>**. Thus, the next complete term of this sequence is <u>H</u>.

56. Each term in this sequence is formed of a number and a capital letter. The number in each term **moves – 2 places every time**:

$$9 \, (-2 =) \, 7 \, (-2 =) \, 5 \, (-2 =) \, 3$$

Hence, the number of the next term of the sequence is **3 (– 2 =) <u>1</u>**. The capital letter in each term **moves – 3 places every time**:

$$B \, (-3 =) \, Y \, (-3 =) \, V \, (-3 =) \, S$$

Hence, the capital letter of the next term of the sequence is **S (– 3 =) <u>P</u>**. Thus, the next complete term of this sequence is <u>1P</u>.

57. Each term in this sequence is formed of a capital letter, a lower-case letter, and a number. The capital letter in each term **moves + 2 places every time**:

$$A \, (+2 =) \, C \, (+2 =) \, E \, (+2 =) \, G$$

Hence, the capital letter of the next term of the sequence is **G (+ 2 =) <u>I</u>**. The lower-case letter in each term **moves + 1 place every time**:

$$b \, (+1 =) \, c \, (+1 =) \, d \, (+1 =) \, e$$

Hence, the lower-case letter of the next term of the sequence is **e (+ 1 =) <u>f</u>**. The number in each term **moves + 2 places every time**:

$$2 \, (+2 =) \, 4 \, (+2 =) \, 6 \, (+2 =) \, 8$$

Hence, the number of the next term of the sequence is **8 (+ 2 =) <u>10</u>**. Thus, the next complete term of this sequence is <u>If10</u>.

58. Each term in this letter sequence consists of two capital letters. The first capital letter in each term **moves – 3 places every time**:

$$Z \, (-3 =) \, W \, (-3 =) \, T \, (-3 =) \, Q \, (-3 =) \, N$$

Hence, the first capital letter of the next term of the sequence is **N (– 3 =) <u>K</u>**. The second capital letter in each term **moves + 4 places every time**:

$$H \, (+4 =) \, L \, (+4 =) \, P \, (+4 =) \, T \, (+4 =) \, X$$

Hence, the second capital letter of the next term of the sequence is **X (+ 4 =) <u>B</u>**. Thus, the next complete term of this sequence is <u>KB</u>.

59. This letter sequence is formed of two alternating series of capital letters. Each term of each series consists of a single capital letter. In the first series of the sequence: <u>A</u>, G, <u>F</u>, D, <u>K</u>, A, <u>P</u>, the capital letters **move + 5 places every time**:

$$A \, (+5 =) \, F \, (+5 =) \, K \, (+5 =) \, P$$

In the second series of the sequence: A, <u>G</u>, F, <u>D</u>, K, <u>A</u>, P, the capital letters **move – 3 places every time**:

$$G \, (-3 =) \, D \, (-3 =) \, A$$

As the next term of the sequence belongs to the second series, the next term will be **A (– 3 =) <u>X</u>**. Thus, the next complete term of this sequence is <u>X</u>.

60. The hidden **four-letter word** is **glum**: A bi<u>g lum</u>bering giant came into view.

61. The hidden **four-letter word** is **them**: I followed <u>the m</u>an until he disappeared.

62. The hidden **four-letter word** is **seen**: The<u>se en</u>igmatic markings are extremely old.

63. The hidden **four-letter word** is **scar**: Ahmed is alway<u>s car</u>eful when using knives.

64. The hidden **four-letter word** is **tent**: The kit<u>ten t</u>ried to catch the butterfly.

65. The two words most opposite in meaning in the two given sets are **<u>brief (adj.)</u>** and **<u>lengthy (adj.)</u>**.
    - **Brief (adj.)** is being very short.
    - **Lengthy (adj.)** is being long.

66. The two words most opposite in meaning in the two given sets are **<u>separate (v.)</u>** and **<u>mix (v.)</u>**.
    - **Separate (v.)** is to set something apart from another thing or things.
    - **Mix (v.)** is to place something with, or in amongst, another thing or things.

67. The two words most opposite in meaning in the two given sets are **<u>apathy (n.)</u>** and **<u>excitement (n.)</u>**.
    - **Apathy (n.)** is a state of a lack of enthusiasm or interest.
    - **Excitement (n.)** is a state of extreme interest or enthusiasm.

68. The two words most opposite in meaning in the two given sets are **<u>insolent (adj.)</u>** and **<u>polite (adj.)</u>**.
    - **Insolent (adj.)** is being rude or impolite to people.
    - **Polite (adj.)** is being well-mannered and courteous towards people.

69. The two words most opposite in meaning in the two given sets are **greedy (adj.)** and **generous (adj.)**.
- *Greedy (adj.) is* being full of greed; being selfish and inconsiderate of others.
- *Generous (adj.) is* being considerate and willing to share with or give to others.

70. The two words most opposite in meaning in the two given sets are **complete (v.)** and **start (v.)**.
- *Complete (v.) is* to finish or to come to the end of something.
- *Start (v.) is* to begin or to commence something.

71. Using the information given, we can deduce which activities each child enjoyed, and, that of all the activities, **hockey was the least popular as only 1 child (*viz.* Susan) enjoyed it**:

Susan	Tarek	Philip	Tom	Julian
Football	Football			
Cookery		Cookery	Cookery	Cookery
Swimming	Swimming	Swimming		
Hockey				
		Rugby	Rugby	Rugby

72. Using the information given, we can deduce which means of transport each child uses to get to school , and, that of all the children, **Sally is the only child who never goes to school on her bike**:

Sally	Mohamed	Dahlia	Peter	Chris
~~Walk~~	Walk	Walk	~~Walk~~	
Scooter	Scooter	Scooter	Scooter	
Bus			Bus	Bus
	Bike	Bike	Bike	Bike

73. A comparison of all four words reveals that only two words begin with the same two letters: D and E, and that two of the numbers begin with the same two digits: 2 and 5. Hence: **D = 2** and **E = 5**. Therefore:
- The code for DELI must be either 2563 or 2537
- The code for DEAL must be either 2563 or 2537

As DELI and DEAL also have the letter L in common and as the only two possible codes for the words have the digit 3 in common, **L = 3**. Therefore, the code for **DELI must be 2537** and the code for **DEAL must be 2563**. Hence: **D = 2; E = 5; L = 3; I = 7; A = 6**. Now we have all the codes for all the letter, **by substitution**, we can deduce that **the code for LIED is 3752**.

74. As we know all the codes for all the letters, **by substitution**, we can deduce that **the code for DALE is for 2635**.

75. As we know all the codes for all the letters, **by substitution**, we can deduce that **the code 3562 stands for LEAD**.

76. As we know all the codes for all the letters, **by substitution**, we can deduce that **the code 2733 stands for DILL**.

77. A comparison of all four words reveals that only two words contain the same letter sequence: TE. Similarly, a comparison of all three numbers reveals that two of them contain the digit sequence: 29. As the letters TE are in the same positions as the digits 29, this means that:
- The **code for MATE is 5629**
- The **code for TEAR is 2964**

Consequently: **M = 5; A = 6; T = 2; E = 9; R = 4**. Hence, **by substitution**, we can deduce that **the code for SEAM must be 3965**.

78. As the code for SEAM is 3965, **S = 3**. Now we know all the codes for all the letters, **by substitution**, we can deduce that **the code for TAME is for 2659**.

79. As we know all the codes for all the letters, **by substitution**, we can deduce that **the code 3962 stands for SEAT**.

80. As we know all the codes for all the letters, **by substitution**, we can deduce that **the code 6453 stands for ARMS**.

PRACTICE TEST PAPER 6: EXPLANATIONS

1. This is a **complex code** which is obtained by moving the letters of the word using the sequence + **1, + 2, + 3, + 4, + 5, + 6, + 7**. Hence, to de-code DQWXFML, the encoding pattern is reversed in the following way: **D – 1 place = C; Q – 2 places = O; W – 3 places = T; X – 4 places = T; F – 5 places = A; M – 6 places = G; L – 7 places = E**. The code **DQWXFML**, therefore, stands for the word **COTTAGE**.

2. This is a **mirror code** where each letter and its code are equal distances from the middle of the alphabet (i.e. the space between M and N). Hence, the code for CALM is found in the following way: **the mirror reflection of C = X; the mirror reflection of A = Z; the mirror reflection of L = O; the mirror reflection of M = N**. The code for **CALM** is, therefore, **XZON**.

3. This is a **complex code** which is obtained by moving the letters of the word – **4 places every time**. Hence, to de-code LKQNO, the encoding pattern is reversed in the following way: **L + 4 places = P; K + 4 places = O; Q + 4 places = U; N + 4 places = R; O + 4 places = S**. The code **LKQNO**, therefore, stands for the word **POURS**.

4. This is a **complex code** which is obtained by moving the letters of the word using the sequence – **3, + 0, – 3, + 0, – 3**. Hence, the code for CUBIC is found in the following way: **C – 3 places = Z; U + 0 places = U; B – 3 places = Y; I + 0 places = I; C – 3 places = Z**. The code for **CUBIC** is, therefore, **ZUYIZ**.

5. This is a **complex code** which is obtained by moving the letters of the word using the sequence – **2, + 4, – 2, + 4, – 2**. Hence, the code for BORED is found in the following way: **B – 2 places = Z; O + 4 places = S; R – 2 places = P; E + 4 places = I; D – 2 places = B**. The code for **BORED** is, therefore, **ZSPIB**.

6. This is a **mirror code** where each letter and its code are equal distances from the middle of the alphabet (i.e. the space between M and N). Hence, YLLI is de-coded in the following way: **the mirror reflection of Y = B; the mirror reflection of L = O; the mirror reflection of L = O; the mirror reflection of I = R**. The code **YLLI**, therefore, stands for the word **BOOR**.

7. This is a **complex code** which is obtained by moving each letter of the word + **6 places**. Hence, to de-code XNESKY, the encoding pattern is reversed in the following way: **X – 6 places = R; N – 6 places = H; E – 6 places = Y; S – 6 places = M; K – 6 places = E; Y – 6 places = S**. The code **XNESKY** therefore, stands for the word **RHYMES**.

8. The first set of words is governed by the following rule:

   o t t e r (r o t a) a l m s
   2 3   1   1 2 3 4   4

   By applying this rule to the second set of words we can see the following:

   a g i n g (?) e l k s
   2 3   1   4

   The letters to be used, therefore, are **a, g, g, e** and need to be re-ordered as: **g, a, g, e = gage**.

9. The first set of words is governed by the following rule:

   r a b b i t (b i t e) s e n d
   1 2 3   1 2 3 4   4

   By applying this rule to the second set of words we can see the following:

   c o p i e s (?) a t o m
   1 2 3   4

   The letters to be used, therefore, are **p, e, s, t** and are to be kept in this order – i.e. **pest**.

10. The first set of words is governed by the following rule:

    f o l l y (l o u d) u s e d
    2 1   1 2 3 4   3   4

    By applying this rule to the second set of words we can see the following:

    m i l k s (?) m o r e
    2 1   3   4

    The letters to be used, therefore, are **i, l, m, e** and need to be re-ordered as: **l, i, m, e = lime**.

11. The first set of words is governed by the following rule:

a b**l**e r (b**e**e t) su**e**t
  1 2   1 2 3 4   3 4

By applying this rule to the second set of words we can see the following:

i g l**o**o (?) s l**a t**
  1 2   3 4

The letters to be used, therefore, are **g, o, a, t** and are to be kept in this order – i.e. **goat**.

12. The first set of words is governed by the following rule:

e d g**e s** (**s e e n**) **n** o r m
3   2 1   1 2 3 4   4

By applying this rule to the second set of words we can see the following:

l i l**a c** (?) **l** e n d
3   2 1   4

The letters to be used, therefore, are **l, a, c, l** and need to be re-ordered as: **c, a, l, l = call**.

13. Using the information given, we can deduce that each child spends the following amount of money on their books:

Jodie	Patrick	Annis	Bilal	Noel
£15.00	£7.50	£14.00	£6.00	£6.00
	(£15 ÷ 2)	(£7.50 + £0.50 + £6.00)		

Therefore:
A. Patrick spends the least ⇨ is not true. Patrick spends £7.50 on his book since his book is half the cost of Jodie's two books which is £15. However, Bilal and Noel each buy a book that costs £6.
B. Three children buy two books each ⇨ is not true. Only Jodie and Annis buy two books each.
C. Only Bilal and Noel share the price of one book ⇨ is not true. While Bilal and Noel each buy a book costing £6, one of the books that Annis buys also costs £6.
D. Patrick's book costs less than Noel's ⇨ is not true. Patrick's book costs £7.50, while Noel's costs £6.
E. Annis spends £14 ⇨ **must be true. Annis spends £8 on her first book (since we are told that it costs 50p more than Patrick's book, i.e. 50p + £7.50 = £8). Annis also buys a book that costs £6. So, in total, Annis spends £8 + £6 = £14.**

14. Using the information given, we can deduce that each of the children enjoy the following video games:

Steve	Ronnie	Monty	Claudia	Liz
			~~Shoot 'em ups~~	~~Shoot 'em ups~~
		Platform	~~Platform~~	Platform
			Role Playing	
F1	F1	~~F1~~	~~F1~~	~~F1~~
FIFA	FIFA	FIFA		

Therefore:
A. Neither of the girls plays FIFA games ⇨ might be true. Although we are told that all three boys like FIFA games, we are not told whether the girls play FIFA games.
B. Neither of the girls enjoys shoot 'em ups ⇨ is true. Neither Liz nor Claudia plays shoot 'em ups.
C. Ronnie always beats Monty at F1 games ⇨ **cannot be true. It is only Ronnie and Steve who play FI games; Monty does not play them.**
D. Steve and Monty are better at platform games than Liz ⇨ might be true. We are not told whether Monty is better than Liz at platform games. Similarly, we are not told if Steve plays platform games, or if he is better at them than Liz if he does.
E. Claudia is Steve's sister ⇨ might be true. We are not told if any of the children are related.

15. The two words most opposite in meaning in the two given sets are **rapid (adj.)** and **sluggish (adj.)**.
   • **Rapid (adj.)** is being fast-moving, fast-acting, or happening quickly.
   • **Sluggish (adj.)** is being inactive or very slow-moving.

16. The two words most opposite in meaning in the two given sets are **read (v.)** and **write (v.)**.
   • **Read (v.)** is to look at and understand the meanings of written words.

- *Write (v.)* is to produce marks such as words, letters, symbols, etc. on a surface, usually a page, that can be read.

17.	The two words most opposite in meaning in the two given sets are **synonym (n.)** and **antonym (n.)**.

- *Synonym (n.)* is a word that has the same meaning as, or a meaning that is very close to, another word.
- *Antonym (n.)* is a word that on certain occasions has the opposite meaning to another word.

18. The two words most opposite in meaning in the two given sets are **dusk (n.)** and **dawn (n.)**.
- *Dusk (n.)* is the time of day after the sun has dropped below the horizon, but while there is still light.
- *Dawn (n.)* is the time of day when light first appears as the sun is rising.

19. The two words most opposite in meaning in the two given sets are **heroic (adj.)** and **cowardly (adj.)**.
- *Heroic (adj.)* is being brave or courageous.
- *Cowardly (adj.)* is lacking in bravery or courage.

20. The two words closest in meaning in the two given sets are **blanket (v.)** and **cover (v.)**.
- *Blanket (v.)* is for one thing to cover another thing, usually completely.
- *Cover (v.)* is for one thing to be placed over another.

21. The two words closest in meaning in the two given sets are **euphoric (adj.)** and **ecstatic (adj.)**.
- *Euphoric (adj.)* is being full of euphoria, extreme happiness, or joy.
- *Ecstatic (adj.)* is being full of ecstasy, extreme happiness, or joy.

22. The two words closest in meaning in the two given sets are **teach (v.)** and **train (v.)**.
- *Teach (v.)* is to instruct someone how to do something.
- *Train (v.)* is to instruct someone how to do something.

23. The two words closest in meaning in the two given sets are **diva (n.)** and **singer (n.)**.
- *Diva (n.)* is a female singer who is very famous, usually (but not always) for operatic singing.
- *Singer (n.)* is a person who sings professionally.

24. The two words closest in meaning in the two given sets are **jug (n.)** and **ewer (n.)**.
- *Jug (n.)* is a deep vessel or container for liquids that has a handle and a spout to aid in pouring.
- *Ewer (n.)* is a large jug that is used for water.

25. Each time, the first number is divided by the third number; then the result is multiplied by 2 to get the second number:
21 (14) 3 ⇨ 21 ÷ 3 = 7; 7 x 2 = 14 ● 30 (20) 3 ⇨ 30 ÷ 3 = 10; 10 x 2 = 20 ● **16 (?) 4** ⇨ **16 ÷ 4 = 4; 4 x 2 = <u>8</u>**

26. Each time, the first and third numbers are added together; then 6 is added to their sum to get the second number:
7 (16) 3 ⇨ 7 + 3 = 10; 10 + 6 = 16 ● 5 (13) 2 ⇨ 5 + 2 = 7; 7 + 6 = 13 ● **9 (?) 5** ⇨ **9 + 5 = 14; 14 + 6 = <u>20</u>**

27. Each time, the first and third numbers are multiplied by each other; their product is multiplied by 2; then 3 is subtracted from the new product to get the second number:
3 (33) 6 ⇨ 3 x 6 = 18; 18 x 2 = 36; 36 − 3 = 33 ● 4 (69) 9 ⇨ 4 x 9 = 36; 36 x 2 = 72; 72 − 3 = 69 ●
8 (?) 2 ⇨ **8 x 2 = 16; 16 x 2 = 32; 32 − 3 = <u>29</u>**

28. Each time, the third number is subtracted from the first number; then the result is divided by 7 to get the second number:
17 (2) 3 ⇨ 17 − 3 = 14; 14 ÷ 7 = 2 ● 65 (8) 9 ⇨ 65 − 9 = 56; 56 ÷ 7 = 8 ● **48 (?) 13** ⇨ **48 − 13 = 35; 35 ÷ 7 = <u>5</u>**

29. Each time, the first and third numbers are multiplied by each other; then 1 is added to their product to get the second number:
15 (46) 3 ⇨ 15 x 3 = 45; 45 + 1 = 46 ● 7 (15) 2 ⇨ 7 x 2 = 14; 14 + 1 = 15 ● **6 (?) 5** ⇨ **6 x 5 = 30; 30 + 1 = <u>31</u>**

30. The completed word in the sentence should read as follows: We always stand up when we sing the national **AN<u>THE</u>M**.

31. The completed word in the sentence should read as follows: We all **GAPED** as Tom calmly removed a scorpion from his arm. The following three-letter words could be used to complete GD: AGE (GAGED); ATE (GATED); ORE (GORED); OUR (GOURD); RAN (GRAND), however, none of these words complete the sentence correctly.

32. The completed word in the sentence should read as follows: I usually get a very **<u>SNO</u>TTY** nose when I have a cold. The following three-letter words could be used to complete STY: PIG (PIGSTY); YEA (YEASTY); CAN (SCANTY); LEE (SLEETY); MAR (SMARTY); POT (SPOTTY); EEL (STEELY); ICK (STICKY); ORE (STOREY); RIP (STRIPY); LED (STYLED), however, none of these words complete the sentence correctly.

33. The completed word in the sentence should read as follows: We need to change the ink **CART<u>RID</u>GE** in the printer.

34. The completed word in the sentence should read as follows: As she was so ashamed of him, Mrs Keller **DI<u>SOW</u>NED** her son.

35. A comparison of the given three numbers and four words reveals that one word has a double letter (i.e. PEER), but that none of the numbers has a double digit. Hence, the missing code must belong to the word PEER. A comparison of the remaining three words and the three numbers reveals that all three words end with P and all three numbers end with 4. Hence, **P = 4**. Comparing the first three letters of REAP, TRIP, and CARP and the first three digits of 3824, 8964 and 5684, reveals only one letter (i.e. R) and one digit (8) are common to all three words and all three numbers respectively. Hence, by matching the positions of R and 8, we can deduce that:
    - The **code for REAP is 8964**
    - The **code for TRIP is 3824**
    - The **code for CARP is 5684**
    Therefore: **R = 8; E = 9; A = 6; T = 3; I = 2; C = 5**. Hence, **by substitution,** we can deduce that **the code for PEER is 4998**.

36. As we know all the codes for all the letters, **by substitution,** we can deduce that **the code for PART is 4683**.

37. As we know all the codes for all the letters, **by substitution,** we can deduce that **the code 8659 stands for RACE**.

38. As we know all the codes for all the letters, **by substitution,** we can deduce that **the code 5649 stands for CAPE**.

39. A comparison of all four words reveals that only two words are made up of the same letters (i.e. LEAF and FLEA). Similarly, a comparison of the three numbers reveals only two of them are made up of the same digits (8769 and 9876). Examining the positions of the letters shows that L is the first letter of LEAF and the second letter of FLEA. A similar examination of the digits shows that 8 is the first digit of 8769 and the second of 9876. Hence,
    - The **code for LEAF is 8769**
    - The **code for FLEA is 9876**
    Consequently: **L = 8; E = 7; A = 6; F = 9**. Therefore, as the remaining code does not contain the digit 9, **the code for CASE must be 3627**.

40. As the code for CASE is 3627, **C = 3; S = 2**. Now we know all the codes for all the letters, **by substitution,** we can deduce that **the code for LACE is 8637**.

41. As we know all the codes for all the letters, **by substitution,** we can deduce that **the code 9637 stands for FACE**.

42. As we know all the codes for all the letters, **by substitution,** we can deduce that **the code 3688 stands for CALL**.

43. Using the information given, we can deduce the amount that each child spends, and, that of all the children, **Samantha spends the least** *(viz. £3.50)*:

Paula	Samantha	Luigi	Dina	Carlos
£4.20	£3.50	£7.00	£6.00	£8.40
(£3.50 + £0.70)	(£7 ÷ 2)	(£6 + £1)		(£4.20 x 2)

44. Using the information given, we can deduce the marks that each child received, and, that of all the children, **Max received the lowest mark**:

Max	Samuel	Elizabeth	Fifi	Gordon
15	17	18	18	16
	(15 + 2)	(17 + 1)	(17 + 1)	(18 − 2)

45. To see the numerical problem, we substitute the letters for their given values:
$$A \times C - B + E \quad \Rightarrow \quad 9 \times 3 - 17 + 7$$
By carrying out the mathematical operations in stages, we arrive at the numerical answer of the problem:
$$9 \times 3 = 27 \quad 27 - 17 = 10 \quad 10 + 7 = \mathbf{17}$$
As the number 17 is represented by the letter B, the answer is **B**.

46. To see the numerical problem, we substitute the letters for their given values:
$$C - D \times E - B \quad \Rightarrow \quad 15 - 11 \times 6 - 13$$
By carrying out the mathematical operations in stages, we arrive at the numerical answer of the problem:
$$15 - 11 = 4 \quad 4 \times 6 = 24 \quad 24 - 13 = \mathbf{11}$$
As the number 11 is represented by the letter D, the answer is **D**.

47. To see the numerical problem, we substitute the letters for their given values:
$$(D^2 - A) \div E \quad \Rightarrow \quad (4^2 - 1) \div 5$$
By carrying out the mathematical operations in stages, we arrive at the numerical answer of the problem:
$$(4^2 - 1) = (16 - 1) \quad 16 - 1 = 15 \quad 15 \div 5 = \mathbf{3}$$

As the number 3 is represented by the letter C, the answer is **C**.

48. To see the numerical problem, we substitute the letters for their given values:

$$E \times A \div C + D \quad \Rightarrow \quad 6 \times 12 \div 8 + 3$$

By carrying out the mathematical operations in stages, we arrive at the numerical answer of the problem:

$$6 \times 12 = 72 \quad 72 \div 8 = 9 \quad 9 + 3 = \mathbf{12}$$

As the number 12 is represented by the letter A, the answer is **A**.

49. To see the numerical problem, we substitute the letters for their given values:

$$(CD + E) - D^2 \quad \Rightarrow \quad (6 \times 7 + 8) - 7^2$$

By carrying out the mathematical operations in stages, we arrive at the numerical answer of the problem:

$$(6 \times 7) = 42 \quad (42 + 8) = 50 \quad 50 - 7^2 = 50 - 49 \quad 50 - 49 = \mathbf{1}$$

As the number 1 is represented by the letter A, the answer is **A**.

50. To see the numerical problem, we substitute the letters for their given values:

$$(4B + BC) \div D \quad \Rightarrow \quad (4 \times 4 + 4 \times 5) \div 6$$

By carrying out the mathematical operations in stages, we arrive at the numerical answer of the problem:

$$(4 \times 4) = 16 \quad (16 + 4 \times 5) = (16 + 20) \quad (16 + 20) = 36 \quad 36 \div 6 = \mathbf{6}$$

As the number 6 is represented by the letter D, the answer is **D**.

51. To see the numerical problem, we substitute the letters for their given values:

$$(D^2 - A) \div 4C \quad \Rightarrow \quad (5^2 - 1) \div (4 \times 3)$$

By carrying out the mathematical operations in stages, we arrive at the numerical answer of the problem:

$$(5^2 - 1) = (25 - 1) \quad (25 - 1) = 24 \quad 24 \div (4 \times 3) = 24 \div (12) \quad 24 \div 12 = \mathbf{2}$$

As the number 2 is represented by the letter B, the answer is **B**.

52. The hidden **four-letter word** is **tore**: "Make sure **to re**member to wash the spoon," Chef said.

53. The hidden **four-letter word** is **coal**: The bucking bron**co al**most threw the rider off.

54. The hidden **four-letter word** is **dash**: After the fire, nothing was left but burnt woo**d ash**.

55. The hidden **four-letter word** is **many**: The tired **man y**awned as he sat on the sofa.

56. The hidden **four-letter word** is **fort**: The children had scones **for t**heir tea.

57. To find the missing letter pair, **RI is a mirror pair (R is the mirror of I); R moves – 3 places to O; O is then mirrored to obtain L ⇨ OL**.

58. To find the missing letter pair, **MN is a mirror pair (M is the mirror of N); M moves + 3 places to P; P is then mirrored to obtain K ⇨ PK**.

59. To find the missing letter pair, **Y moves + 8 places to G and V moves – 3 places to S ⇨ GS**.

60. To find the missing letter pair, **J moves + 3 places to M and V moves – 1 place to U ⇨ MU**.

61. To find the missing letter pair, **B is mirrored to obtain Y; D is mirrored to obtain W; the resultant mirror pair YW is then inverted to obtain WY ⇨ WY**.

62. **Smoke** and **ash** are the odd ones out because they **are the products of fire**, whereas fire, flames, and blaze are synonyms.

63. **Conversely** and **however** are the odd ones out because they **are adverbs that are used to introduce contradictory information**, whereas thus, hence, and therefore are adverbs employed to introduce a reason or a cause.

64. **Bang** and **bruise** are the odd ones out because they **are actions that do not break the skin**, whereas slash, cut, and lacerate are actions that do.

65. **Pencil** and **stylus** are the odd ones out because they **are writing implements that do not require ink**, whereas Biro, fountain pen, and quill do.

66. **Will** and **could** are the odd ones out because they **are modal verbs**, whereas future, past, and present are the names of three verbal tenses in English.

67. **Brass** and **steel** are the odd ones out because they **are alloys**, whereas gold, silver, and lead are metals.

68. **Army** and **navy** are the odd ones out because they **are two military bodies**, whereas shield, protect, and guard are synonymous verbs meaning to keep safe from harm.

69. The only two words that form a proper word when combined are **in** and **vest** to give **invest**. Ontop (on + top) is an incorrect spelling of the phrase 'on top'; attop (at + top) is an incorrect spelling of 'atop'.

70. The only two words that form a proper word when combined are **eye** and **lid** to give **eyelid**.

71. The only two words that form a proper word when combined are **as** and **king** to give **asking**. Soking (so + king) is an incorrect spelling of 'soaking'.

72. The only two words that form a proper word when combined are **air** and **less** to give **airless**. Breatheless (breathe + less) is an incorrect spelling of 'breathless'.

73. The only two words that form a proper word when combined are **am** and **bled** to give **ambled**. Ammid (am + mid) is an incorrect spelling of 'amid'.

74. Each term in this sequence is formed of a lower-case letter, a capital letter and a number. The lower-case letter in each term **moves according to the pattern – 4, – 3, – 4**:

$$r\,(-4=)\,n\,(-3=)\,k\,(-4=)\,g$$

Hence, the lower-case letter of the next term of the sequences is **g (– 3 =) d**. The capital letter in each term **moves according to the pattern + 6, + 2, + 6**:

$$B\,(+6=)\,H\,(+2=)\,J\,(+6=)\,P$$

Hence, the capital letter of the next term of the sequence is **P (+ 2 =) R**. The number in each term **moves according to the pattern – 2, – 3, – 4**:

$$15\,(-2=)\,13\,(-3=)\,10\,(-4=)\,6$$

Hence, the number of the next term of the sequence is **6 (– 5 =) 1**. Thus, the next complete term of this sequence is **dR1**.

75. This letter sequence is formed of two alternating series of capital letters. Each term of each series consists of a single capital letter. In the first series of the sequence: X, Y, A, D, F, G, I, the capital letters **move according to the pattern + 3, + 5, + 3**:

$$X\,(+3=)\,A\,(+5=)\,F\,(+3=)\,I$$

In the second series of the sequence: X, Y, A, D, F, G, I, the capital letters **move according to the pattern + 5, + 3**:

$$Y\,(+5=)\,D\,(+3=)\,G$$

As the next term of the sequence belongs to the second series, the next term will be **G (+ 5 =) L**. Thus, the next complete term of this sequence is **L**.

76. Each term in this letter sequence consists of three capital letters. The first capital letter in each term **moves according to the pattern + 1, – 3, + 1**:

$$I\,(+1=)\,J\,(-3=)\,G\,(+1=)\,H$$

Hence, the first capital letter of the next term of the sequence is **H (– 3 =) E**. The second capital letter in each term **moves – 4 places every time**:

$$J\,(-4=)\,F\,(-4=)\,B\,(-4=)\,X$$

Hence, the second capital letter of the next term of the sequence is **X (– 4 =) T**. The third capital letter in each term **moves according to the pattern + 2, + 4, + 2**:

$$K\,(+2=)\,M\,(+4=)\,Q\,(+2=)\,S$$

Hence, the third capital letter of the next term of the sequence is **S (+ 4 =) W**. Thus, the next complete term of this sequence is **ETW**.

77. Each term in this letter sequence consists of two capital letters. The first capital letter in each term **moves according to the pattern – 1, – 0, + 1, + 2**:

$$M\,(-1=)\,L\,(-0=)\,L\,(+1=)\,M\,(+2=)\,O$$

Hence, the first capital letter of the next term of the sequence is **O (+ 3 =) R**. The second capital letter in each term **moves according to the pattern + 1, – 3, + 1, – 3**:

$$O\,(+1=)\,P\,(-3=)\,M\,(+1=)\,N\,(-3=)\,K$$

Hence, the second capital letter of the next term of the sequence is **K (+ 1 =) L**. Thus, the next complete term of this sequence is **RL**.

78. Each term in this sequence is formed of a single capital letter. Each time, the capital letter **moves according to the pattern + 3, + 2, + 1, + 0**:

$$D\,(+3=)\,G\,(+2=)\,I\,(+1=)\,J\,(+0=)\,J$$

Hence, the capital letter of the next term of the sequence is **J (– 1 =) I**. Thus, the next complete term of this sequence is **I**.

79. Each term in this sequence is formed of a number, a lower-case letter, and a capital letter. The number in each term **moves according to the pattern – 1, – 0, – 1**:

$$6\,(-1=)\,5\,(-0=)\,5\,(-1=)\,4$$

Hence, the number of the next term of the sequences is **4 (− 0 =) 4**. The lower-case letter in each term **moves according to the pattern + 0, + 1, + 0**:

$$k (+ 0 =) k (+ 1 =) l (+ 0 =) l$$

Hence, the lower-case letter of the next term of the sequence is **l (+ 1 =) m**. The capital letter in each term **moves according to the pattern + 4, + 2, + 4**:

$$C (+ 4 =) G (+ 2 =) I (+ 4 =) M$$

Hence, the capital letter of the next term of the sequence is **M (+ 2 =) O**. Thus, the next complete term of this sequence is **4mO**.

80. Each term in this letter sequence consists of two capital letters. The first capital letter in each term **moves according to the pattern + 2, − 1, + 2, − 1**:

$$A (+ 2 =) C (− 1 =) B (+ 2 =) D (− 1 =) C$$

Hence, the first capital letter of the next term of the sequence is **C (+ 2 =) E**. The second capital letter in each term **moves according to the pattern + 0, − 1, − 2, − 3**:

$$B (+ 0 =) B (− 1 =) A (− 2 =) Y (− 3 =) V$$

Hence, the second capital letter of the next term of the sequence is **V (− 4 =) R**. Thus, the next complete term of this sequence is **ER**.

CHALLENGING WORDS LIST

Ambled (v.) *is the past simple form of the verb* 'to amble' *which is* to walk or move in a slow or relaxed way. (6.73)

Anthem (n.) *is* a song (usually one that is uplifting) that is associated with a specific group, cause, country, etc. (6.30)

Aside (adv.) *is* 1. to be apart. 2. to one side. (4.62)

Aside (n.) *is* words spoken (often in a play) that are not intended to be heard by another person (often on the stage). (4.62)

Cartridge (n.) *is* a container for bullets, ink, tape, film, etc. (6.33)

Crank (n.) *is* an instrument that looks like a handle which is bent in two places at right angles (often used in the past to start the engine of a motor car). (4.31)

Disown (v.) *is* to deny, or to refuse to keep, a connection with a person. (6.34)

Drab (adj.) *is* being dreary or dull. (4.27)

Dram (n.) *is* a small unit (often of an alcoholic drink). (5.33)

Gage [or gauge] (v.) *is* to measure, estimate, or assess something or someone. (6.8)

Glum (adj.) *is* being in low spirits. (5.60)

Impotent (adj.) *is* being extremely weak or powerless. (5.68)

Inert (adj.) *is* being inactive, unmoving, or in a state of rest. (5.68)

Invest (v.) *is* to spend a lot of time, energy, effort, or money on something because you expect a worthwhile result. (6.69)

Lunge (v.) *is* to make a forward, sudden thrusting movement. (5.32)

Oats (n.) *is* the name of a cereal that is often used as a type of breakfast cereal as well as an ingredient in biscuits, cakes, etc. (5.7)

Omen (n.) *is* an event or thing that is seen as a sign of something happening in the future which could be good or evil. (5.7)

Plod (v.) *is* to walk, move, or work slowly. (4.53)

Rein (n.) *is* a strap that is attached to a horse's bridle that is used to control and guide the horse (usually used in the plural: reins). (4.74)

Swaddle (v.) *is* 1. to bandage something. 2. to wrap something (often a baby) in pieces of cloth. (4.72)

Tad (n.) *is* a small or tiny amount of something. (5.34)

Whizz [or whiz] (n.) *is* a whistling sound. (5.8)

Whizz [or whiz] (v.) *is* to move through the air quickly. (5.8)

Zany (adj.) is being crazy in an entertaining, funny way. (5.8)

Zone (n.) is an area of a city, country, etc. (5.8)

MORE 11+ VERBAL REASONING TITLES BY STP BOOKS

You might also be interested in

Help your child become a spelling wizard with this comprehensive spelling workbook!

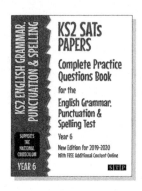

Give your child the edge with this unique collection of ALL the different questions used in the actual SATs grammar tests from 2015-2019!

Make practising English grammar, punctuation and spelling fun for your child with this collection of 18 bite-size 10-minute tests!

Boost your child's confidence and spelling skills with this bumper collection of 30 SATs-style Spelling Tests!

Give your child a head start with this volume of 4 complete, fully UP-TO-DATE SATs grammar tests!

Help your child become an English expert with this comprehensive grammar, punctuation, vocabulary and spelling workbook!

Printed in Great Britain
by Amazon

44149334R00031